The Inner Game
of Selling Yourself

James Borg holds a BSc (Econ) degree from the
London School of Economics (LSE), where he
also studied psychology. After university, a career
in advertising, sales and marketing saw him
achieve record-breaking results in a highly
competitive environment. A member of the
prestigious Magic Circle, specialising in 'mental-
ism' (ESP/mind-reading effects), he attributes his
success to simply 'getting inside the mind' – something, as the book clearly shows, that we are all
capable of doing. As a consultant with a post-
graduate degree in Psychology, he advises on
marketing techniques and the application of
psychology in the workplace, and contributes to
newspapers and magazines.

The Inner Game of Selling Yourself

*Build your mind-power to
boost your influence*

JAMES BORG

VERMILION

London

1 3 5 7 9 10 8 6 4 2

Copyright © James Borg 1989

James Borg has asserted his right to be identified
as the author of this work.

First published in Great Britain 1989
by Heinemann Professional Publishing Ltd

New edition printed in the United Kingdom in 2000 by Vermilion
an imprint of Ebury Press
Random House, 20 Vauxhall Bridge Road, London SW1V 2SA

Random House Australia (Pty) Limited
20 Alfred Street, Milsons Point, Sydney,
New South Wales 2061, Australia

Random House New Zealand Limited
18 Poland Road, Glenfield,
Auckland 10, New Zealand

Random House South Africa (Pty) Limited
Endulini, 5A Jubilee Road,
Parktown 2193, South Africa

The Random House Group Limited Reg. No. 954009
www.randomhouse.co.uk

A CIP catalogue record for this book is available from the British Library

ISBN 0 09 185602 7

Printed and bound in Denmark by Norhaven A/S, Viborg

Papers used by Vermilion are natural, recyclable products
made from wood grown in sustainable forests.

Cover design by Slatter-Anderson

It's never too late to become
who you might have been.

Foreword

Has it ever occurred to you that you can get almost nothing of any significance done without the help of others? Whether you are a grand panjandrum or a humble teaboy – or something betwixt and between – you rely on your colleagues, friends, workmates and subordinates. You can advise, recommend, give orders or offer to help, but every one of those involves other people. Even individuals who work individually – like journalists and barristers – continually rely on others. In today's extraordinarily complex world, the simple words of the great sixteenth-century poet John Donne ring truer than ever: 'No man is an island'.

So the more successfully you can communicate with other people, the more successful you will be. You must communicate with people in ways that will persuade them to do what you want them to do without more ado.

To do this, you must first persuade them that what you have to say is important, and worthwhile, and helpful, and realistic. *The Inner Game of Selling Yourself* will show you how to communicate in ways that will do all those things. It will, quite simply, help you ensure that, when you speak, people listen – and act.

Anyone who cannot communicate soon gets known as a bumbler. If all the people in the world who don't know how to sell themselves knew how their colleagues and friends mocked and mimicked their waffle, they would rapidly sharpen their thoughts. *The Inner Game of Selling Yourself* will show you how to put yourself and your thoughts across convincingly – in the simplest and most effective ways possible.

Read on.

Winston Fletcher

A key figure in British advertising, Winston Fletcher has founded and led some of the UK's top agencies and is a former President of the Institute of Practitioners in Advertising as well as Chairman of the Advertising Association. He is the author of *Tantrums and Talent – How to get the best from creative people* and eleven other books, has regular columns in national newspapers and magazines and is currently Communications Director for Foote Cone & Belding Europe.

Contents

1

Get inside the mind
and you will find

When we use the term 'selling yourself', and it creeps into a variety of situations these days, we're talking about something that everybody has to put into practice all the time. It's probably better recognised as trying to get other people to do or give something, trying to get a point across or get somebody to agree to a course of action.

Most people inhabit two worlds simultaneously. There is the world of our personal life and home. Then there is the other world, that of work, in an office, shop, studio, factory or wherever it takes place. Good communication and interpersonal skills that are cultivated to enhance your work effectiveness will also help you in your personal life. By the same token a lot of the skills you develop to help you in your personal life are invaluable in boosting your success in the world of work.

Every day, in your personal life or at work, you may come into contact with people who need to understand your point of view, whether it be for you to help *them* or equally for them to help *you*. In the workplace you'll find individuals, of varying status in the hierarchy, 'selling' their ideas to others. Their ultimate aim is the same: getting their viewpoint or message accepted. You see people in discussion, from the boardroom to the rest-room, trying to influence one another to agree to a course of action. The successful ones are those who use subtle techniques of persuasion. Their reasoning strikes a chord in the mind of the other(s) and so an idea is accepted.

Despite all the practice, few perform this art to its best effect. Yet it's so simple. It requires no special skills, but just draws upon a few basic personal qualities. Most organisations have a product, service or cause to sell to the outside world. How effectively this is done determines the future of the organisation, its employees and ultimately the economy. Companies cannot exist unless those employed to sell their product go out and persuade people to buy. And without buyers there would be no personnel departments, no production departments, no salary departments or indeed any departments.

You would think that with such a paramount role to play in business, and in life in general, there would be more emphasis and training on our 'interpersonal' and 'communication skills'. In the past, perhaps the fault lay with the companies themselves. Too much emphasis was placed on employing anybody prepared to swot up on features of a product or service. Then they would be let loose under the company's banner. No regard was paid to the personality of the individual and their ability to market themselves. Employers were no doubt impressed by a candidate's ability as a fast talker. But there's no place for this in today's highly professional environment – where perhaps being a 'fast listener' would be a far more worthwhile quality.

The message gradually seems to be getting through now. Selling yourself is essentially about appealing to human nature.

After all – we're dealing with individuals. The game of selling yourself is therefore an *inner* one, played in the minds of the participants. The successful person uses all their resources to *get inside the mind* of the other person and resolve a conflict, effect a sale, persuade the other person to accept a point of view, or whatever, drawing out enough information to tailor the proposition into a winning one.

It's using the *art of gentle persuasion* to achieve an outcome that brings mutual benefit. And this means recognising the workings of what psychology refers to as the 'conscious' and 'subconscious' mind.

The fact is that messages are mostly decoded in the other

person's (the receiver's) unconscious mind, which tends to interpret things on an *emotional* level. By carefully choosing the right words to plant in the mind, the seeds are sown to achieve a positive effect. The receiver's conscious mind should automatically accept the ideas put over – and that increases the chances of a positive outcome.

The all-seeing, all-knowing 'persuader' is aware that outside influences can inhibit the effectiveness of their communication and therefore a favourable outcome. He can sense when attention is straying and can recognise the effect that certain interruptions will have on the other person's concentration. He thus compensates for the effects of major disruptions on his presentation. He readjusts the pace to keep in time with the other person.

In all occupations you will find that the selling of the 'self', and how effective this is, determines the degree of success that the individul or organisation enjoys. Even the professions such as solicitors and accountants have come round to realising that sharpening interpersonal skills is now not only necessary, but also productive, in the face of increasing competition. These practitioners have always sold their services but have not necessarily regarded themselves as being in the marketplace and selling a service. (What's the difference between a solicitor or accountant trying to engage a client, in the face of competition, for some house-purchase or taxation work, and a landscape gardener offering his talents in a particular area?)

So they have mostly been content to offer their services in a passive way: 'You (client) come to me and *you* make all the effort. I'm the "expert", and so I don't need to engage in any "selling of the self".' Think of your own experiences. Hasn't the relationship with any of these practitioners been *mutually* of more benefit when they've taken the time and trouble to get inside your mind? Hasn't communication been more effective, productive and maybe more 'human'? Thankfully, the situation is gradually changing and more attention is now being paid to 'people skills'.

Even doctors have now been told to wise up on their interpersonal skills with patients, in response to growing complaints over the last few decades. They constantly have to *persuade* patients to take a particular course of action. Nevertheless, on the receiving end of this 'caring' profession, we've all been subjected to the indifferent, unempathetic manner of a general practitioner or private doctor in the consulting room or at the bedside.

So an appreciation of good communication techniques is essential for everybody. Whether at work or in everyday life, the techniques of handling and understanding people are fundamental to our ultimate well-being. There's always a need to win over other people for one reason or another: your neighbour's a little bit unhappy about the sycamore tree that's started to encroach over his fence. He wants it cut down completely; you'd just like to have it trimmed back. Your best friend would like to house-sit for you while you're on holiday – she's got a reputation for being untidy and fond of wild parties. The computer repairman who gave you a twelve-month warranty on his repair – it's now fourteen months and it's defective, but you've only used it four times since the repair. The list is endless. As you begin to think about it for yourself, scores of examples will no doubt occur to you. In each case, getting inside the mind of the other person is vital. But few people make the effort. If they did, the results would be spectacular.

It only requires a keen awareness. If this comes naturally, you're in a minority – but probably a successful and content minority in both the social and the business contexts.

As we enter the twenty-first century with the increasing dominance of digital technology, a subtle realisation is now in evidence. All that extra human time spent in front of electronic screens has exacerbated, but – on the more positive side – also highlighted the *deficiency* of human skills. Less exposure and interaction with people and more intimate encounters with the computer monitor have increased skills in the latter area, at the expense of the former. Employers are now placing a premium on 'people skills'.

The goal of this book is to awaken this awareness within you. Drawing upon the science of psychology and its applied aspects, you'll be able to sharpen your inner skills and have more fun in life.

What's the secret? *ESP*.

2

Mind-bending using ESP: Empathy, Sincerity and Perspicacity

ESP

So what are the mental techniques for getting inside the other person's mind? ESP! We're talking about a variation on the theme of extra-sensory perception (apologies to aspiring spoon-benders!). This ESP demands different qualities:

E Empathy
S Sincerity
P Perspicacity

Empathy

This is the magic personal quality that is at the root of success in communicating with others. If you've got it – *exploit* it! If you haven't – *develop* it!

What is it? Put simply, it's the ability to read emotions in others. It's being able to experience another person's perspective. From an emotional point of view, even if you have not experienced a similar state of affairs, you are still able to empathise and know how another feels. Application of this important quality is essential in all areas of life: in a work context, you can see how important it would be in the areas of sales and management, for example; politicians yearn to project this quality; parents have to develop this skill to a fine degree; and if you're trying to improve on your success with the opposite sex – see what happens when you don't have it!

Empathy means *putting yourself in the other person's mind; feeling with them; understanding how what you say will affect them; being sensitive to their problems; getting in tune with them.*

This will involve constantly tailoring your approach and what you say to different people because you're treating them as *individuals*. They are all different. Your job is to find out what they are thinking and show understanding. Your empathy enables you to spot different types of people and almost get inside their minds to find out what will satisfy them, worry them, inspire them. In short: what factors might or might not push the relationship further.

We're talking about what separates the good from the mediocre. If, for example, in your job you have an impressive knowledge about a product or service that you are selling but lack empathy, you certainly won't do as well as somebody who has both.

Have you ever been in a restaurant where one waiter inspires you to order more (or more expensive!) dishes, whereas another waiter has the opposite effect? A clothes store where one assistant leaves you walking out with a multitude of carrier bags and another's 'Can I help you?' precipitates your exit? The hotel receptionist who responds with: 'I'm sorry the room's not to your satisfaction' and you feel she really means it? An understanding of human nature and a curiosity about people are all that this involves.

Some people have this innate sense to a very high degree. So they use it successfully. They're almost able to predict how another person will react to something. They put themselves on a similar wavelength, so they know what to say and how to say it.

But if you haven't got it, at least be *aware* of it. Then *develop* it.

Sincerity

If you're going to develop empathy, you must show sincerity. But being sincere is not enough. Ultimately empathy is based on trust, and this is one of the most difficult social skills to understand and convey. Think about it in terms of general relationships. The first crisis that often occurs in any relationship is when two individuals no longer trust each other. Everything that we do either promotes or lessens the trust within a relationship. It is not a stable personality trait that we possess, as it is constantly changing.

To put it more succinctly: trust occurs *between* people and not *within* people. Some people are more trusting than others, and some people are inherently more trustworthy; but it's the conveying to the other person that's important.

Some people emit true sincerity without effort and so the other person's trust level is high. It can usually be spotted instantly. It's indefinable; it's just there. You know it when you see it. Because it is heartfelt: it shows in the face, in the eyes. So if you are a sincere person, it probably comes naturally.

If you consider you are sincere but it doesn't seem to come across, relax: lose yourself in being interested. When you show genuine sincerity – that you actually care about someone's problems, be it a friend, relative, work colleague, or buyer of your product – you're elevating yourself to a higher plane. The conversation takes on a different tone; the other person is more receptive to your questions and tells you more. This helps you steer a discussion in the direction that you want. A certain amount of trust has been established. (Remember: trust exists in relationships, not in someone's personality.)

You can convey acceptance of another person's thoughts and ideas and also propose different ideas and viewpoints. There doesn't have to be agreement with everything the other person says. It's being trustworthy that advances the relationship. The more supportive you are of the other person, the more likely it is that they will disclose their thoughts, ideas and feelings to you. And it's a circular relationship because the more trustworthy you are in response to these 'self-disclosures', the deeper and more personal will be the thoughts the person shares with you. This occurs as much in a business context as it does in private life. So if you want to increase trust, you have to increase your trustworthiness.

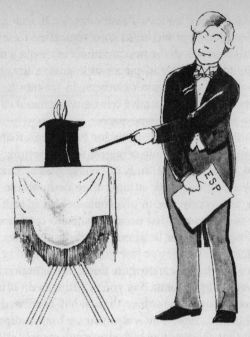

Perspicacity

This is really an ingredient of empathy. It's the part that allows you to see into the other person's mind. It means having insight.

Such keen perception comes not only from applying the mind but also from using two of our senses: looking and listening. This means that virtually everyone has a built-in potential for perspicacity.

The problem is that because they're so wrapped up in themselves, many people don't apply it often enough. They fail to observe non-verbal behaviour and other tell-tale cues. They may sense something about the person they are inter-acting with *subconsciously* – but that piece of perception is not registered and so is not put to good use.

It's not used to further one person's understanding of and rapport with another. In the case of non-verbal messages, which are fraught with ambiguity, the receiver often finds it difficult to be sure about what the sender is feeling. These messages are more powerful in communicating feelings than are verbal messages in the making of accurate judgements.

It is by taking bits and pieces of cognitive data that we form an overall impression of others. In seeking to explain another person's behaviour, we rely on two general categories of causes: situation and disposition.

Situational causes are reasons for behaviours that rest on the demands or constraints of a given social setting. Certain situations induce certain kinds of behaviour. For example, if you're checking in people at an airline desk, where there is normally an orderly queue of people behaving in a patient manner, and a disgruntled person rushes to the front of the queue complaining that he's been waiting in the other line for twenty minutes and they've just closed the desk, so he's going to miss his flight, we can attribute this to the situation and not to the man's temperament. Say you're sitting in an office with a prospective client – an office that he has borrowed from a colleague, with a time-limit – and you see him surreptitiously (well, not that surreptitiously, because you spotted it!) checking his watch all the time. The reason may be situational rather than him thinking you're a bore (or the fact that he's an impatient person).

In other situations, a person's behaviour will stem from *dispositional* causes. These are behaviours that are determined by that individual's personality traits and characteristics. Some people are aggressive, friendly, anxious, lively, etc., by nature, regardless of the situation. Therefore, when they behave in an agressive, friendly, anxious or lively manner, their behaviour is probably due to their disposition.

Self-presentation

Psychologists say that we engage in self-presentation (or 'impression-management') during social interactions: we regulate and control the information we present to others, in an attempt to create specific, generally positive impressions of ourselves. Many people are quite happy in any social situation and can blend in with anybody present. By contrast, others appear oblivious of social norms and maintain the same behaviour in each and every situation. The differences between these two types of people reflect differences in 'self-monitoring'. This term is used to describe the regulation of a person's behaviour to a particular situation or the expectation of others – in other words, how one presents oneself.

As you would expect, *high self-monitors* adapt well according to the situation, and are concerned about the 'right' behaviour; they are anxious to conform to how others expect them to behave and skilful in changing their behaviour to what is appropriate for the social situation.

Low self-monitors are insensitive to the social demands of a particular situation, and have a clearer sense of themselves.

A lot of research has been done highlighting the differences between the two groups. It was found that high self-monitors are more interested in finding out information about others; they also remember it better. In personal relationships they are more friendly and less anxious. High self-monitors are concerned with responding in an appropriate and productive manner in any given situation. They are sharp enough to make accurate assessments of the right behaviour for the setting.

Which is the best way to act? The answer obviously depends on one's values and the appropriateness of the situation, whether at work or in personal life. In practice, both high and low monitors can lead satisfactory social lives, with an appropriate balance. In the context of work, in some roles the high self-monitor's style is more appropriate, and in other, more 'principled', roles the low self-monitor would fare better. Which one are you? You meet both types all the time so it is useful to recognise them in others as well as yourself.

We all try to present ourselves in positive ways – at job interviews, when we meet new people, at work functions, when persuading people to buy things from us. Why do we do this? We are motivated to make good impressions. Psychological findings show that we try and make our behaviour match what we can term our 'ideal self', supporting the view we have of ourselves. In addition, we self-present in order to 'audition' different selves, our aim being to choose an identity that we can incorporate into our main identity. So other people are not only the audience of our self-presentations; on many occasions, we too want to *witness* the impact of our own behaviour for our own benefit.

We also engage in what's known as 'audience-pleasing' which, in essence, is designed to make the audience (of one or more people) feel good. We want others to experience a positive reaction to us, either from a genuine desire to please others ('Haven't seen you for ages, Carol. Like your hair.') or to try to persuade others to behave in a particular way ('You're a distinguished gourmet, Miss Smith. You'd probably appreciate our daily flown-in Maine lobster – it's on the special menu.').

For some people, the word 'persuasion' has ominous undertones. But throughout this book, when we use the term, we're talking about the art of gentle persuasion – subtle techniques that work on the mind to produce a desirable result. We all have an aversion to the feeling of having been manipulated. That's not what this book is about. It's about bringing out two types of intelligences that some psychologists have identified:

Interpersonal intelligence: an understanding of other people – how they feel, their likes and dislikes, their motivations. The person with these abilities can almost predict how others will act, and is therefore able to interact with them effectively. In life, you'll notice that successful politicians, sales people, psychotherapists and people with highly developed social skills are possessed of this kind of intelligence.

Intrapersonal intelligence: the ability to have insight into our own thought processes, feelings and emotions, and an awareness of the causes and consequences of our actions, which in turn allows us to make the right decision.

Possession of these qualities enables us to get inside the minds of other people and be effective in our communication with them.

3
Being a good listener

Effective communication is at the core of our whole existence. Being able to communicate effectively is the foundation for advancement in all types of relationships, both professional and personal. This interpersonal communication is quite often described as a message sent by one person to another (the receiver) with the purpose of affecting the receiver's behaviour. You might say to someone: 'That's the third train cancellation this week' as you glance up at the timetable at Waterloo Station, with the aim of eliciting the reply: 'Shocking, isn't it?'

In this limited form, this creates a basis for communication: it's simply the way we speak and listen to other people. What prompts any form of communication is the desire for another person to know what we know, to value what we value, to feel what we feel and to decide what we decide. Of all the aspects of communication that we engage in, listening is perhaps the most important.

Think back to when you were a baby; listening was the first language skill you developed. In the divorce courts and in the workplace, a breakdown is often attributed to poor listening. If it is carried out effectively, it creates and improves personal relationships.

To get inside the mind, you need to master the fundamentals and importance of good listening skills. In every situation in life, *effective* listening will help you to understand another person's thoughts, feelings and actions.

When people are accused of being poor listeners, it is usually done behind their backs. So they remain unaware of this major failing, which can lose them friends, work colleagues and business clients.

How do *you* rate as a listener? Being a bad one is a very serious sin of which most people are guilty. They only *think* they listen. The compulsion to speak in very many cases devalues the function of listening. Fact: most people prefer talking to listening. Unfortunately, they usually exercise this preference.

Active listening is difficult. It requires a lot of concentration. But it has to be mastered. It is fundamental to learning. The sad thing is we were never taught at school about the importance of listening skills. Even now, more emphasis is placed on logarithms than on listening.

You often hear of somebody talking too much. Nobody could be accused of *listening* too much! It's surprising what people will tell you if you're a good listener. Think how it works among friends and acquaintances on a social level. What were you like the last time you bumped into your neighbour in the street or when you were having dinner with friends? In families you'll constantly hear that there's a listening problem. Beleaguered parents will say that the children don't listen and children will be exasperated because their parents don't listen to them. Since listening is a sign of affirmation, it promotes self-esteem and the opposite usually occurs if there is a breakdown.

In business it's no different. People are drawn to a good listener. There may be a definite appeal in being able to talk to somebody outside the internal politics of their own company who listens objectively. A person bogged down in the red tape of their own position may relish the therapeutic satisfaction of getting something off his chest to an outsider.

It pays good dividends if you listen. It can establish you as a 'friend'. And that makes for more mutual understanding in a business relationship.

Besides, if you listen carefully you pick up all sorts of information about the idiosyncrasies of the company – and the individual you are dealing with! People who are poor listeners often see listening as a passive – and therefore unproductive – activity. Their *ego* gets in the way. They feel the need to be talking in order to make any impact with the other person.

Observe people in internal meetings in the workplace and you'll see the talk-talk-talk syndrome with a vengeance. There are those who continually interrupt with superfluous remarks. It makes them believe that they're contributing. They'll miss important points through butting in. And they'll ask questions to which they already know the answers. But they're communicating, they feel, because they're talking. How wrong they are! Attentive listening is also part of communication.

You'll quite often see the above scenario in sales situations. Never monopolise the conversation. Let the other person speak and then, at an opportune moment, take the reins. It has to be give and take. Talking long and loud doesn't always equate with having personality; it is often a substitute for it.

Productive listening

There's only one way to listen productively: try to remove all distractions from your mind so you can concentrate on the speaker – easier said than done! Such distractions come from your *thoughts*, *senses* and *emotions*. Preoccupation or lack of interest impedes effective listening.

If you're not interested in what the speaker has to offer, you'll have an aversion to listening. Preoccupation with something can be a barrier, too. For example, if someone has just bumped into the back of your car, the nuisance of it keeps coming back to you.

The environment can also influence how well we listen. Have you ever tried to have a meaningful discussion with somebody when there's a TV set blaring in the background? Your requests to have it turned off because you want to discuss something might meet with a reply such as 'It's OK, I can listen even if it's on.' You might achieve a compromise with the other person agreeing to turn the sound off and leave only the picture on. It doesn't work. You're still distracted by the visual 'noise', even though the auditory interference has been eliminated. Noise can come from all sources. It's difficult to concentrate in a meeting if there are roadworks going on out-side. Equally, you could be in a seminar and miss the first twen-ty minutes of what is said through being absorbed in a beauti-ful oil painting hung over the fireplace (visual noise again).

So who are you trying to kid when you claim to be a good listener? Listening isn't merely saying nothing while the other person is talking. It means *hearing*. And that's what people find difficult.

We think much faster than we can speak

There's a major obstacle to effective listening that we all have to contend with: *We can think much faster than anyone can speak*. Tests have shown that:

1 We talk at between 120 and 150 words per minute.
2 We think at the rate of 600–800 words per minute.

Result: since we can think at approximately *five times* the rate that somebody is speaking, we tend to think of other things and not just what is being said.

Of course, the figures vary, but the fundamental point is that the listener is always ahead of the person doing the talking. The implications of this are evident. When listening to people, the radio, television, etc., your mind has time to wander away from the words being spoken. So you lose concentration. And if you start thinking about something and it takes you over, you'll blot out the other noise and so switch off. You may look as though you're listening but you're not actually hearing anything.

Since all communication between individuals essentially either moves the relationship *forwards*, *backwards*, or *keeps it the same*, the way you listen and respond to other people is paramount in promoting the relationship. If you listen empathetically, you're giving out the signal: 'I'm interested in everything that you're saying and I'm eager to understand your point of view', and if you fail to listen and respond in the right way, you're saying the opposite.

So how do we get the best out of the speaker by showing that we're listening in the right fashion?

Don't interrupt

Because thoughts formulate faster than speech, there's a strong temptation to interrupt the other person. It's a sign either that you're not listening, or that you're eager to sidetrack the speaker's line of reasoning (in favour of your own), or that you are one of the many people who enjoy talking more than listening. Whatever the reason, you may antagonise the other person. They're less likely to listen intently to you (when they've got to do the listening!) if you cut them off midstream. The spontaneity is gone once you've interrupted. Consider this example:

First neighbour to second neighbour: 'You know, I've been thinking about the problem of your new extension blocking the light from our bedroom. I know it's been approved by the council and you've got planning permission. I don't want us to fall out . . .'

Second neighbour (interrupting): 'Look, its OK, I've been to see the architect and I've told him to reduce the height. It's sorted out. Sarah didn't want any bad feeling. Neither did I.'

First neighbour: 'But I meant . . .'

Second neighbour: 'It's fine, honestly. Don't think any more about it. I've got to dash – I'll get stuck in the traffic on the M25. Bye.'

Well. If the second neighbour had listened without interrupting, events would have taken a different course. His neighbour was going to say: 'We're having a loft conversion done – been toying with the idea for years. Sue suggested we make that our new bedroom, as it's much bigger and faces south, and so your extension won't be a problem for us.'

Don't finish the other person's sentences

As we saw in the previous example, one person's interjection turned out to be detrimental to his cause – he'd have been much better off if he had kept quiet and let his neighbour finish. Another irritating habit – if it's done repeatedly – is to finish the speaker's sentences. Consider the following:

Client: 'And so this time I want to avoid any . . .'

Designer (interrupting): 'Further catastrophe?'

Client: 'Er, yes. That's right.'

Designer: 'Don't worry. We'll pull out all the stops.'

You can do this occasionally, but don't make a habit of it. To keep doing it to the same person is not only irritating but it is also bad psychology, because the speaker will not feel in control of his own ideas.

Filling in words for somebody on the odd occasion can show that you are actually listening and provide feedback that you are attentive, but it can also get in the way of the other person's ego. It may well look as though you're trying to wrestle original thoughts from him and claim them for your own. That renders you suspect, and will not help the rapport that you're aiming to establish.

There's another drawback to jumping the gun like this: you may easily guess the *wrong* ending! Perhaps that possibility has never occurred to you, simply because nobody has ever bothered to correct your mistake.

Maybe the other person doesn't want to embarrass you and tell you that you're an idiot who has messed up their line of thought. Because they can't do that, they can't continue with their original point (and it may have been crucial).

The ending that you so kindly supplied (i.e., the wrong one) may implant doubts that never previously existed. For example:

Dan (the client): I'm happy to do business with you – it's a couple of years now, I think, since we dealt with you – but I want to make sure . . .'

You (interrupting): '. . . that you don't get the wrong consignment like you did the last time, and have to wait another three weeks.'

Ouch!

What Dan was actually going to say was: 'I want to make sure . . . that the purchase order form that we'll send you gives the different delivery locations for each batch.'

What's happened is that the client is alerted to the fact that your company messed up the delivery last time, which caused a five-week delay. He may not have known anything about it or may have just forgotten. You've just told him. Now he has doubts because late delivery could cost his company a lot of money and bad feeling within the organisation. Dan decides to think about it – 'I'll get back to you.' He never does. Business has been lost because of a throwaway and ill-considered line.

To make matters worse, what your client was actually going to say was to your benefit.

Remember the old adage: '*Better to keep your mouth shut and be thought a fool, than to open it and remove all doubt!*'

Talking over the other person

Another bad habit adopted by many people is talking over
the other person while they are speaking. You may think of
members of your family who are guilty of this, or friends or
work colleagues. Your boss may do it to you all the time. It's
very common. And it's very irritating when you're on the
receiving end. It says: 'I don't care what you're going to say,
my story's better than yours (or bigger and better than yours
– remind you of the school playground?). For example:

Anne: 'Did you enjoy the cruise Charlotte? How was it?'
Charlotte: 'Oh, I can't tell you how much we enjoyed our-
    selves. Do you know, they had food on each deck at almost
    all hours of . . .' (what she says next is completely drowned
    out by the other person) '. . . the day and then there were
    midnight buffets and unfortunately we got a touch of food
    poisoning on . . .'
Anne (talking over): 'We went on a fabulous cruise. Now
    when would that have . . . ? Oh, I know, it must have been
    ten, no, more like eight and a half years . . .'

Do you recognise this tendency in yourself? Or do you recognise it in other people? We all talk over others to some extent,
for various reasons, not evident at the time, such as excite-
ment, a desire to show empathy, or a desire to 'bring someone down' (if they're obnoxious!). If we're aware of it, we can
at least *try* to avoid doing it. It can lose you friends and it can
lose you business.

So the message is clear, whether it's you doing the listening
or whether you want somebody to listen effectively to what
you say: try to avoid or prevent any barriers to productive listening.

Offering advice too soon

This is often a problem when you're eager to help someone,
whether it be a friend, a colleague or somebody in a business

situation. You want to offer support and help so you jump into the conversation quickly. The result is that there's an abrupt and premature end to the two-way conversation. If you're the classic 'problem-solving' type, you may be guilty of this and if you're the type that oozes empathy, you may also do this frequently. It comes from a desire to help.

(a) That's twice he's telephoned at the last minute, saying he has to work late. I'm concerned; the thought crossed my mind that he might be seeing someone else. I don't know whether I'm just being silly . . .'
   'Ditch him. He's not worth it.'

(b) 'You see, our problem is the staff just don't stay. Maybe after four to six months they . . . I don't know whether it's the attitude of our senior people towards them. Or, I don't know, there could be a few other reasons . . .'
   'Don't worry. We vet all applicants thoroughly. Our company's been around for ten years now. I'm sure we can get some stability for you.'

The problem in both of these examples is that the quick response has blocked any further lines of enquiry. Although they hadn't finished, the speakers were cut off and now the conversation is being guided in the listener's direction. The speakers had more to get off their chest and have been cut short.

Psychologists in the field of therapy are coming to realise that all too often their clients aren't heard because therapists are doing therapy *to* them rather than *with* them. This extract from a therapist's notes is quite illuminating:

What I myself found important, but extremely difficult, to do was to try to listen to what clients say instead of making up meanings about what they say. Just listen to what they say . . .

Conversational questions come from a position of not knowing and are the therapist's primary tool. They involve responsive or active listening, which requires attending to the client's stories in a distinct way, immersing oneself in clients' conversations, talking with them about their concerns, and trying to grasp their current story and what gives it shape . . . the questions are not formed by the therapist's preconceived theories of what the story should be . . . Conversational questions are, therefore, not generated by technique, method or a preset template of questions . . .

Each question . . . comes from an honest, continuous therapeutic posture of not understanding too quickly, of not knowing.

Paraphrasing

Listening empathetically is the key to advancing interpersonal relationships. The technique of paraphrasing is very powerful, as it lets the speaker see the ideas (and feelings) they have conveyed, from the other person's point of view. When you paraphrase, you are not adding to the message, you are sending back the meaning you *received*. The listener is effectively telling the speaker, using their own words, what they interpret from what has been said. It is invaluable because:

1 The sender is reassured that the listener is trying to understand the basis of their thoughts and feelings, and appreciates being heard.

   (a) 'Let me just clarify what you're saying. You're a bit concerned about a stranger having your flat keys, and that's the main reason.'
   'Yes exactly.'

   (b) 'It looks as though what you're saying is you'll place your television advertising budget with us as long as there's no conflict of interest with another client.'
   'That's correct.'

2 The listener may want to ensure the sender hears what they have just said (this could be for a positive or a negative reason) as this will give them a clearer perspective of the implications of their current line of thinking.

   (a) 'At the moment it looks as though you're saying that you want to give up the classes altogether. You realise that if you change your mind later, you'd have to start from scratch again – is that what you want?'
   'Well . . . no, I suppose not.'

(b) 'Can I just clarify what I think you're saying? You'd like your IT managers to try the system out piecemeal. It would end up costing you four times as much this way. Would that be acceptable to the departmental managers?'

'Mmm . . . that's something to consider.'

3 The listener may have found it difficult to gauge the other person's *true* feelings, and needs to try to attain an accurate understanding of what has been said.

(a) 'I'd just like to ask you if I've understood this correctly. You want to change departments because the gossiping interferes with your work. That's it, is it?'

'Well, there are other things.'

(b) 'Can I just be sure of this in my own mind? It's the fact that he doesn't ever ask how you are that makes you feel this way?'

'No. That's just a small part of it – it's the tip of the iceberg.'

We cannot overemphasise the importance of *listening* in our family life, work situations and friendships. It pays enormous dividends. Of course, we want people to listen to us too, so our questions are important, as are getting and holding attention.

4

Holding attention

We want people to listen to our message, so we have to keep our audience – whether it be one or two people or two hundred – interested enough to listen. Furthermore, we want to keep their *attention*. Most of us have short concentration spans, for various reasons.

It's very difficult to keep interest level constant. Attention is held only when interest is *rising*. In the last chapter, we spoke about the problem of the mind allowing itself to engage in competing thoughts (because we can think at a faster rate than the rate at which a person typically speaks) while seemingly paying attention to something else. Sure, we're 'hearing' – but we're not listening. Most people assume the two actions are complementary. But they're not – as this overheard conversation illustrates:

'What did you do at the weekend, then?'

'Drove down to the coast with the kids, to Brighton, and stayed overnight.'

'Oh, Brighton. I haven't been there for years. Did you take the train?'

'No, I drove there.'

'Did you go on your own?'

Zzzzzzzzz . . . Disastrous! The questioner was not truly listening. He edited the conversation until he found a key word that sparked his interest – and then of course he missed all the other details. The rest were words he had chosen just not to register. Go on, admit it to yourself. You do it all the time, don't you? At home; when you're with your friends; in shops; at work; when you're interviewing an applicant for a job position; in business meetings; while you're watching television; in the theatre – in fact, *just about wherever you are*!

People fool themselves into thinking that they're good listeners. They're probably good hearers, but that doesn't allow them to take interest in, and thus make use of, what they are told to further their romantic relationships, their friendships or their dealings at work. The wife says to her husband, who's sitting in an armchair looking at the television, remote control in hand:

'You will mow the lawn for me tomorrow, won't you?'

'What? Oh yes, yes.'

'We've got to get to the theatre by seven, so we ought to leave now.'

'Yes. OK, OK.'

'I was going to wear this dress – d'you think it makes my bottom look big?'

'Yes, yes.'

'What? You think it's big?'

'What? No! I mean no.'

'You just said "yes" to everything. If you'd unglue that remote from your hand . . . You don't listen to anything I say.'

Ouch! What probably makes this situation even worse is that although her partner was looking at the television, he was probably only hearing and not listening to the sound. He was listening to his own thoughts in his head. We're all constantly 'running our own tapes'.

How can we encourage people to listen to us? How can we gain their attention, keep their attention? By keeping them interested in what we have to say, so that they won't get bored and start listening to *themselves*.

Actors know very well that their success in the West End, on Broadway, in a local theatre or even in a school play depends firstly on one thing: maintaining audience attention.

Their aim is to make interest rise for the maximum length of time and try to prevent it falling. They have to compete with the audience's own mental distractions, let alone any visual distractions. A lapse of attention by a member of the audience during a 'boring' scene may let in all sorts of extraneous thoughts:

> Mmm. I hope the car will be all right parked where it is. It was sticking out from the corner a bit. Not my fault. Why do they need double yellows that far round a corner? They're a bit trigger happy, those wheel clampers around here. If Sue's aunt hadn't phoned we wouldn't have been late. Why do people always . . . We could have got into the car park if it wasn't for her. Still, it's now a lot nearer than the car park. I hope I can find it later. Oh yes, I know. It's near that pizza place. They do nice pizzas there. Maybe we'll eat there later. Now, have I got my cheque-book? No, Sue's got it in her handbag. What's that thing on the edge of the stage? Oh, it's a revolver. I wonder if she knows she's got a big hole in her stocking . . . ?

By the time they try to get back into the swing of the play they find they've lost interest and it's hard to regain it.

Attention breakdowns

This problem exists all the time in everyday life. Let's take a typical business situation, for example. You're visiting a prospective client's office (Note: this could equally well be a job interview, a consultation with a private doctor in Harley Street, just about any kind of 'meeting' – the problems are the same):

You enter the client's office and take the seat offered. After a few pleasantries you begin your presentation. Three minutes into your spiel, his telephone rings.

'Do excuse me for a minute,' he says, taking the call.

After two or three minutes, when he has finished, he turns back to you: 'Now, where were we? I'm sorry. Please carry on.'

You recall where you left off and continue talking. The client nods as you are speaking and you feel that he's with you.

About two minutes later his secretary walks in.

'Excuse me,' she says to both of you, and then addressing her boss: 'Would you just sign this, please? It's very urgent.'

He apologises to you and stares at the cheque. He questions his secretary about a certain point relating to the amount on the cheque. He then asks her to locate some paperwork from the files. She leaves.

You pick up your thread and afterwards ask the client some questions. He's speaking now. Five minutes on, the secretary returns with some documents. Apologises to you again, as he studies various bits of paper. He seems disturbed by something he is reading; pensively he picks up his pen, signs the cheque and hands it over. She leaves the room.

You now realise that there is a breakdown of attention here. He's definitely not with it now. It's certainly not furthering your cause. You're wasting your breath. You can barely remember what you've said; what hope for him? However, you carry on. A woman enters with two cups of coffee.

Halfway through your preamble, your client's phone rings. More apologies. It's his boss wanting some figures for the departmental meeting in fifteen minutes time. He puts the phone down and starts fumbling through his in-tray.

'Do carry on talking,' he says to you, as he flicks through sheets of paper searching for the required report. He doesn't find it. He looks defeated.

'I'm sorry. One of those days. Keep talking. But could I ask you to be brief?'

Brief?!

This is a frustrating scenario, but quite a common one. Most of us have experienced it (or subjected somebody to something similar). During a job interview, a meeting with the boss to discuss something important to you (or to the boss), a meeting with a client, during a sales presentation. This scenario knows no bounds!

The point: *It's difficult to control attention when there isn't any in the first place*.

The above example highlights what happens in varying degrees in many meetings and interviews. There is a breakdown of attention which is totally beyond our control.

It would be better, at the point of being asked to be brief, to call a halt to the proceedings (depending on the circumstances, of course). You could suggest returning at another time, when the other person is less likely to be distracted and/or under time pressure.

To continue under such unfavourable circumstances is a waste of time and effort; the other person's mind is elsewhere. A hurried discussion is fair to neither party. Try the suggestion of making another appointment. The inconvenience involved may not seem worthwhile, but if you're determined to get a 'message' through, it's preferable. Also, you've helped the other person out of a tight spot. The next time you should at least receive more sympathetic attention.

Keeping the audience's attention or interest is probably the bedrock of any successful conversation or meeting. Everything else follows from that. *No attention = no communication = no result*. But most people fail to recognise when somebody's attention is wavering. It's up to you to pick up the signals and act accordingly.

The problem is this: when presenting an idea, demand, request, sales pitch or whatever, it's usually crucial to get the point across at the first attempt – assuming conditions are conducive. This initial discussion usually shapes the eventual outcome. Having rejected an idea in the first instance, most people do not like to change their minds later – even if they know they're wrong. It's sometimes a question of pride. They may not want to look indecisive or as though they were incapable of making the right evaluation in the first place.

Suppose you're making a sales pitch. Who wants to waste a good presentation (and more importantly, time) on somebody whose mind is simply not there? If your proposal is only half heard then your chances of success are reduced by 50 per cent immediately. So if you want somebody to buy your product, to agree to your request for next Thursday off, to accept your proposal of marriage, or your reasons for handing in your resignation, you need their full attention. Otherwise it's better to try to defer the conversation. Remember: *you usually get only one chance.*

The numerous interruptions experienced in the situation just described can be analysed to show the possible effect on the client's receptiveness; in other words, how the disturbances affect his attention span.

1 In the first three minutes your client absorbs most of what you say.
2 The telephone rings. His mind is now on the subject of the telephone conversation (the advertising agency wants to know whether to amend the copy for the new advertisement: could he call them back by 3 pm?). He puts the phone down when he's finished the call.
3 You go on talking and he nods repeatedly (thinking to himself, while 'listening', 'Mmm, maybe we should have spot colour for the logo on this new ad . . .').
4 His secretary brings a cheque to be signed. He's not satisfied and asks her to return with some supporting documents.

5 You resume where you left off – you can just about remember this yourself – and he listens. (But he's thinking: 'How could the cheque be for that much? They must have made an addition error on their invoice. I'll ask Joanna to . . . I know, I bet they're trying to sting us for . . .')

6 You ask him a question relating to the Internet software, but he's not prepared; he's on the wrong track. That's because he's missed most of what has been said.

7 The secretary returns with some documents. He reluctantly signs the cheque.

8 You begin to talk – but now you can almost see the client's 'wheels' turning ('I should have queried that invoice with the suppliers; their bills never show a meaningful breakdown. Our financial director's really going to give me a hard time at the departmental meeting . . .'). But all the time he's nodding away in acknowledgement of what's being said.

How deceptive. But it's up to you to look for the signs. You can tell by the person's eyes and their expression whether their mind is elsewhere. If you know you've lost their attention, it's better to stop.

The attention curve

Audience attention is best represented as a curve. Maintaining a steady rise is virtually impossible. The ideal curve would be very hard or impossible for anyone to attain (see Figure 1).

The curves are more likely to be formed with intermittent waves: attention is gained, falls away and is then built up again (see Figure 2).

Fact: people are always losing the thread of a conversation (we're all human!) and need something explained again. But they won't *admit* it. There are numerous reasons for this:

1 They don't want to seem impolite.
2 They don't want to look stupid.

3 They feel guilty for letting their minds wander (in other words for 'two-timing' you).
4 They have decided they're not interested and they 'switch off'.
5 They don't want to prolong the meeting because they have another engagement lined up; or they've just got a lot to do.

If this happens to you, it's your responsibility to take corrective action to try and regain the person's attention.

Programme your mind to retain an attention curve, to be applied in any meeting situation. This will allow you to

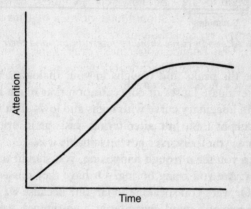

Figure 1 *Ideal attention curve: attention is held and maintained right from the start*

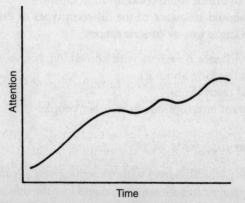

Figure 2 *Typical attention curve, with intermittent waves*

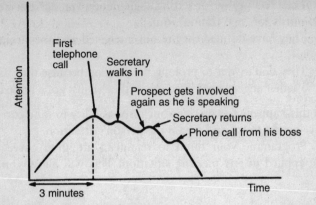

Figure 3 *Attention curve showing interruptions and their effect*

visualise the peaks and troughs in your dialogue. You'll be able to evaluate lapses of concentration that much better by seeing an imaginary curve with highs and lows. You may find it difficult at first, but after trying this out in appropriate situations, you'll discover how invaluable it is.

When you see a trough happening, you should try to find out why. Are you being boring? Or have they missed a main point? Or were you speaking in jargon? Because we can't see another person's mind engaging in 'two-timing', we have to look for the giveaway signals, or be alert and understand enough to notice when concentration lapses.

You should be aware of the different types of distractions that can cause loss of concentration:

1 Your listener disagrees with something you've said (and starts thinking about it).
2 Visual distractions.
3 Constant interruptions from other people.

Listener disagrees

Somebody who disagrees with something you've said may go off at a tangent in their own mind and lose the thread of what you're saying:

'Of course, I think he's too inexperienced to make a good Prime Minister. The other fella . . . Well, I know he's got his . . .' *(Listener disagrees and their concentration lapses.)*

'Well, you had the opportunity to make your feelings known before you started dating him. See, when I was your age our mothers told us . . .' *(Listener disagrees.)*

'I have to say, Mr Mills, I think you'll find that quick, responsive service facilities should be of more concern to you than durability . . .' *(Listener disagrees.)*

In some cases, if you've said something that your listener strongly disagrees with, he may just be waiting for the earliest opportunity to end a conversation or to terminate a meeting. Anything you say is wasted.

Visual distractions

A visual distraction is anything that triggers our overactive minds, forcing us to blot out a 'message' coming across to us.

1 You're watching *Hamlet* in the theatre and you notice that Ophelia is wearing a watch. The distraction is so great for a few minutes that you miss the dialogue and artistry.
2 You're with a prospective client in a restaurant; he suddenly spots somebody he knows seated in the far corner. He constantly looks away to see if that person has noticed him; you can see his attention wavering.
3 If you're talking to somebody who has a stain on his jacket, or a prominent button missing with the loose thread hanging, that can be enough to distract your mind in following the gist of any conversation.

So, if for example you rip your sleeve on the reception filing cabinet coming in, or lose a vital button in the car park and are aware that you look untidy, tell the other person. His knowing that you know should be enough to stop his mind wondering about the offending flaw. Case closed.

Equally, if there's to be a meeting in your office and there are potential visual distractions there, try to anticipate them. Turn the Pirelli calendar the other way round!

I'm reminded of a true instance recounted to me many years ago by a work colleague. Going to see a prominent advertising agency he was greeted by warm smiles as he waited in reception; even those people leaving the building smiled at him warmly. He was impressed with the friendliness of the company. When he was shown into the office of the account director he was seeing, the whole meeting was punctuated with further warm smiles, from all those present. He left the office, thinking to himself how well the meeting had gone – they were all so friendly, full of smiles.

Even the taxi driver who took him back to his own company's offices was smiling the whole time. When he got back to work, popping in to the WC first, he glanced in the mirror to comb his hair and on his face, to his horror, he noticed four small bits of blue toilet tissue that he had stuck over his cuts after shaving that morning! I know – you're dying to ask – did he get the business from the advertising agency? No. They didn't hear a word he said!

Dealing with constant interruptions

It's annoying when you're having a conversation with somebody and you're constantly interrupted. You're in a restaurant with a friend, excitedly telling her about the new job you've just got, and the waiter keeps coming and interrupting you, even though you've said you'll let him know when you're ready for coffee. You're giving a colleague at work some instructions on how to operate a complicated system and a junior clerk repeatedly interrupts you, asking unimportant questions.

In the workplace, it's unproductive when you're with a boss, colleague or a client on their home ground, if your conversation is continually disturbed. The attention curve for the earlier example that we analysed is shown in Figure 3.

But as the working environment becomes increasingly pressurised, the above scenarios are all too common. With people taking on more and more, 'downsizing', open-plan offices, etc., few meetings are completely free of interruptions. You have to live with it. Unfortunately, the onus is usually on you (with a message to impart or an idea to sell) to detect a breakdown of attention and carry out the salvage operation.

If the disruption is in human form you can at least categorise the nature of any problem involved because you hear what is said. You can then evaluate its possible effect on your listener's concentration.

With a telephone distraction, you have to try to observe the other person's facial expressions and check the tone of voice if the conversation turns monosyllabic. The reasons could be, for example:

1 Their boss calling to give them a dressing down.
2 Their partner announcing they're leaving.
3 Their secretary informing them that their car has just been clamped.
4 An irate client threatening to cancel a sizeable contract.
5 Their son phoning to say he's dropping out of university.
6 Production department telling them that delivery for a major client will not go out on time as originally promised.

Unless they refer to the phone call, you'll have to guess the likely level of distraction from their eyes and tone of voice. If they look mildly or seriously preoccupied, what is the answer?

Repeat. I repeat: *repeat*. Give him a summary of what you said before the interruption.

People are always concerned about sounding parrot-like in their discussions. But consider this: research continually shows that *people only take in about 40 per cent of what they hear*. (And that's without interruptions.)

So, by recapping, you're increasing your chances of making your point stick.

After an interruption, visualise the mental attention curve and pick up on the points made before you were silenced. You can do this briefly. The other person's new problem has blotted out part of what you said earlier, so you're helping them *to come back into the discussion*. You're into their mind and working out where the breakdowns have occurred. Rescue the discussion – and save the situation.

By summarising what you've said, each time, you're also helping the other person to crystallise all the benefits that you've been discussing. In the case of a job interview, for example, all may not be lost as you encapsulate to the interviewer your worthy achievements and capabilities. If you're there making a sales pitch, you're doing the same thing: restating the benefits you referred to earlier. Besides, by being able to extract the salient points of your presentation, you're showing that your line of thinking is logical and structured. It enhances your stature.

It's impossible to get totally undivided attention as long as the other person is capable of engaging in stray thoughts (this applies to all of us). It does help, though, to *recognise* how supplementary thoughts caused by interruptions and distractions can defocus your own presentation. If we know how to recognise it, we can at least do something about it.

Ways to win more attention

Change the seating if possible

This principle applies everywhere, but let's take the workplace setting as an example, where a desk quite often separates the sender and receiver of a message. The person whose desk it is cannot get away (mentally or physically) from the piled-up proof on his desk of all the work awaiting him.

So what? Anybody having a discussion from behind their desk is bound to be all too aware of the paperwork waiting there to be done. You know from your own experience: it's there in front of you, reminding you of how *busy* you are. ('In fact, I'm so busy, what the hell am I doing talking to this person?') This allows all sorts of random thoughts to enter the head: 'Mmm. I must remember to write a reply to that letter; oh I must get that out by Friday; what's that green bit of paper there? Oh no, I forgot to renew that subscription . . . Hey, Fran's spelt "analysis" wrong on that memo.'

It's a consequence of being on your own territory. You can see your workload grow in front of your eyes, bringing distraction with it. A vague anxiety sets in. It's not fair on the other person.

You should be aware of this territorial problem. If you've experienced the desk-bound type before, you would be wise to *try* to get them out of the hot seat to a calmer corner of the room – in other words, away from the desk. Take the lead in changing the scene.

Avoid breaks

Awareness of the attention curve reminds you that the best possible situation is to sustain attention on that upward curve as far as you can. Given that we decide on most things on an *emotional* basis, it follows that timing is all-important to catch the fleeting emotion that says: 'Yes, I'm happy to offer you the job' or 'Tell me more' or 'OK we'll try out your product – we'll give it a go' or 'yes, you can have the day off on Wednesday'. Anything that lowers that momentary emotional high can turn a decision the other way.

So it's up to you to keep the other person's attention on that incline and not to break the spell.

Imagine you've been watching a film on TV for the last forty-five minutes. The car is now twelve feet from the edge of the cliff and the handbrake cable snaps; it's rolling down towards the edge! *Click, click*: commercial break.

When the film resumes after three minutes, do you still have the same feeling? That feeling of sustained drama that had you concentrating intently for three-quarters of an hour? The suspension of disbelief that had completely engrossed you and stopped your own mind wandering for the duration of the film? The short answer to these questions is 'No'. The break has forced you to lose that state of high emotion. The spell is broken.

It's no different in interpersonal situations. You've been discussing a possible promotional campaign with a managing director for half an hour or so. She's quite interested, it appears.

'Have you got some more case-studies you can show me?' she asks.

'Yes, I'll just dig them out from my case.'

You pick up your case and start to search. As it's taking such a long time, the MD turns to some memos on her desk. She has the courtesy to look up three minutes later, but as you're still searching frantically, she carries on attending to her own work.

'Ah, this is it – no, that's . . . Wait, I think this is a good example. No, sorry. I've got it somewhere here.'

Of course, eye contact has been lost for some time now. You've been too busy on a paper chase. The MD's emotional state has shifted now. Her acceptance level is starting to slip, as well as her confidence in you. Her thoughts are now turning to the letters she has to sign, where she's meeting her friend for lunch and why she shouldn't proceed with your proposition.

Eventually, the sheets of paper are located.

'Let me see now. There were three concurrent campaigns in different regions in this example. The costs are calculated differently in this case . . .'

Out comes the calculator: more lost eye contact.

'Well, that doesn't seem right. Maybe I pressed the minus instead of . . . No, I couldn't . . . I wonder if the battery . . . ?'

Two to three minutes of calculator malfunction follow. Nothing is as boring as watching people tap away at calculator keys (second only to watching paint dry), especially when you don't have confidence in their dexterity.

By now our bored decision-maker has lost that 'high' and has all but come down to earth with a bump. This is not an unusual situation. It happens all the time.

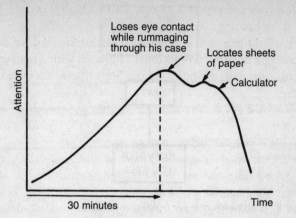

Figure 4 *Example attention curve. For thirty minutes there is good attention, then attention falls sharply*

It's important to analyse the situation. It's not that the potential client doesn't think the proposition is a good one. It's just that the feeling of wanting to go ahead has gone. She'll think about it and perhaps pursue it in the future, avoid a gamble at the present time.

The lesson? Recognise that because most decisions of acceptance – for anything – are made on an emotional level, it is important to get acceptance when feeling is running high.

So avoid interrupting your discussion or presentation by taking your eyes away from the other person. If you do that, you give them licence to 'stray'. Have your props at hand. If you need to use a calculator, do it slickly.

The attention curve for this example would look something like Figure 4.

Say what you're going to say

We can perhaps call this the golden rule for holding attention and making your message memorable and understood: 'Say what you're going to say. Say it. Say what you said.'

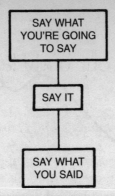

Figure 5 *The golden rule for holding attention*

First, you're telling your audience what you will be speaking about. If it's a subject of interest (and of course you would make sure it is), it keeps people interested. Then you actually tell them about it. Finally, you recap on what you've actually said.

On the basis that most people only take in about 40 per cent of what they hear, this formula increases our chances of being heard.

5

Mind your body language

The mind and body are one

Of course, communication is more than just speaking and listening. We also express feelings in a *non-verbal* fashion when we're engaging in both of these activities:

1 You talk to somebody and you're sending a message to them both verbally and non-verbally.
2 They receive the message, interpret it in a certain way and send back to you a message that is both verbal and non-verbal.
3 You respond to their reply in a verbal and non-verbal way.

The process continues. We're all at it! In fact, the work done by psychologists over the years continually puts a figure of around 40 per cent for verbal and 60 per cent for non-verbal meaning in a typical face-to-face conversation with another person. What does this tell us? It indicates clearly that for optimum interpersonal success we need to be more aware of non-verbal behaviour than what is said. That is to say, that we judge actions quite separately from speech as a guide to a person's *inner* feelings.

The impression you make and the ones you receive are greatly influenced by your non-verbal behaviours.

We can note three main purposes of body language:

1 When it's used *instead* of speech.
2 When it's used to *reinforce* speech.
3 When it displays (or betrays) a person's *mood*.

When it comes to meeting people for the first time, the research carried out by social psychologists emphasises the importance of first impressions and the impact that is made

41

in the first few minutes. This applies to our social and our professional life. We take in all aspects of a person's appearance, from their personal characteristics to their clothes and body language. Of course, this is hardly error-free. Rather, it should alert us to what occurs in everyday life, what we should do when we observe and also what happens when we ourselves are the subject of observation.

In every encounter with another human being our moods and emotions at that point in time are exhibited (for potential analysis) to discerning others: they can be perceived in the posture, position and movement of our bodies. Nobody can be expected to share our subjective inner thoughts. They are, after all, private property. And yet we are able to pick up various emotions in others and can communicate our feelings to them: the traffic is two-way if both parties are empathetic.

The term '*body language*' is often used to describe our non-verbal behaviour. Its role in interpersonal communication is of paramount importance. Without saying a single word, you are conveying an impression with your own body language.

We're used to seeing shocking statistics in the newspapers every day. Now prepare for another shock. 93–7 or put another way 7–38–55.

In a face-to face encounter, 93 per cent of the impact of your message is non-verbal and only seven per cent of the impact of your message is verbal.

There's a further sub-division: of the 93 per cent non-verbal communication, 55 per cent is body language and 38 per cent relates to non-verbal aspects of speech – this is termed *paralinguistics* – the tone of voice and related cues; in other words, the vocal changes or variations in the voice. It is important to look at this interesting area of paralinguistics since it forms such a high percentage of communication. It relates to:

1 *Volume*: loudness or softness will depend on what we are trying to convey. We may add emphasis to words by speaking more loudly (or the opposite).

2 *Rate of speaking*: this can affect the amount of understanding the audience receives. For example, somebody
who speaks really fast may lose the listeners' attention.
Equally, a slow speaker can make the audience lose
interest.

3 *Tone, pitch and inflection*: a person's pitch can go from
low to high, and in the course of everyday conversations
we'll adjust our pitch and alter our inflection. For example, you'll observe that a lot of people have a rising pitch
when they're asking a question. Skilful use of tone, pitch
and inflection can enhance your message positively.
Remember what you are conveying through natural variation. See how changes in emphasis affect these identical
statements – does each convey the same meaning?

You want me to go?
You want *me* to go!
You want *me* to go!

We said earlier on that body language plays a great role in
supporting our words; *paralanguage* plays an equally important part, whether it's adding a negative or a positive slant to
our words. It gives words meaning and makes for a more
effective speaker.

Working for you or against you?

It may be deliberate on your part – to give a certain impression – or it may be just the way you are. Much of our body
language is learned and then turns into habit over the years.
But the important thing to consider is this: is it working *for*
you or *against* you?

Sarah: 'So I really don't know whether to splash out on the
Aga in case the sale falls through.'
Jane: (chin resting on right hand, rubbing eyes repeatedly)
'Yes. I know.'
Sarah: 'I mean, look what happened to Liz in Personnel after
she had her offer accepted . . . I mean . . .'

Jane: (staring to the side and then looking down at her coffee cup) 'Well, I know.'

Sarah's thinking: 'Jane's not interested in my problems. She's jealous because I'm getting a new house and she's stuck in her two-bedroom flat.' It could be that Jane had lost sleep the night before for some reason, and was not feeling too good and so displayed body language signs of lack of attentiveness. If that's the case, there has been a misinterpretation of the message. With damaging consequences.

It's so important to be aware of how you may appear to others because body language – being 'silent' in its delivery – does not elicit a reply if the message has been wrongly interpreted. In the above example Jane did not mean to give an impression of inattention, but Sarah received this silent message. Another scenario:

Mr Simpson: 'Do sit down, Mr Caine. You've brought the files with you, I take it?'

Mr Caine: 'Yes, I've got them here.' *(Sits down, looks at watch pointedly, looks up at Mr Simpson, then stares at his own shoe at the end of his tapping foot.)*

Mr Simpson: 'I felt that if we just went through the figures together, we could agree on how we can change the budgets next year so that nobody loses out in significant terms.' *(Leans forward slightly and maintains eye contact with a smile.)*

Mr Caine: 'That's OK by me.'

Mr Simpson: 'I've got a simplistic breakdown here. If we take just one person from your department we'll cut down on the salaries budget by enough to take space at the exhibitions in Bath and Geneva. What do you think?'

Mr Caine: 'If that's what we have to do, so be it.' *(Starts to pull fluff off his jacket, graduating down to his trousers.)*

Mr Simpson: 'But how do you really feel about this. Tell me, because it has got to be a joint decision. I may even bring Mr Henson in on this.'

Mr Caine: 'Fine by me. I take it you don't mean whoever goes has to go immediately?' *(Continues searching for fluff and has now reached his left sock!)*

At this point Mr Simpson politely makes up an excuse to terminate the meeting under the pretext of having just remembered that he had to get something done for head office. Everything about Mr Caine's body language had shown disagreement. And Mr Simpson showed enough perspicacity to pick up the signals.

There could have been a reason for Mr Caine's mood that day or a more important underlying reason for his disapproval. Either way, it would probably have been unwise to continue the meeting in the hope of a productive outcome. The two individuals could at least go away and think about it and possibly seek third-party advice or whatever. Mr Simpson could make enquiries to try and find out any hidden concerns on the part of Mr Caine.

Using empathy to pick up signs of body language

So it is imperative that if we're to enjoy success in the game of selling ourselves in our personal and work life, we are as concerned with our non-verbal cues as with our verbal ones. Feelings are displayed better by non-verbal messages. The outward signs of people's internal emotional states are their facial expressions, body movements and gestures, postures, touching, tone of voice and other behaviours.

Facial expressions obviously do much to communicate feelings. It is the face that is the most revealing in terms of non-verbal behaviour (as well as the eyes). We interpret other people's emotions and their attitudes towards us initially from their facial expressions. Research shows that there is a universal recognition of several facial expressions. We are quite successful at recognising six different emotions that are displayed on the human face:

sadness	surprise
disgust	anger
happiness	fear

The fact that the expression of these emotions has proved to be universal, spanning the whole cultural spectrum, has led to the conclusion that it is inborn rather than learned. However, it is relatively easy to regulate and control our facial expressions.

A lot can be said with the face. We use facial expressions in everyday life to communicate feelings to other people. If someone says something we disagree with, or we believe they're telling a lie, or if they've said something that's embarrassing to another person, without saying a single word, we can give a 'look' that conveys our message to them. We also use our faces to reinforce a verbal message that we may be giving. But we have to be cautious. We often hear the expression (and use it ourselves): 'It's written all over your face'; but we know how easy it is to conceal our true feelings. Have you ever watched the losing nominees at the 'Oscars' applaud the winner as they clutch the trophy? If we make our judgements based *only* on facial expression we can be extremely inaccurate in judging emotions.

Observation shows that human beings physically mimic the actions of others in certain situations to convey understanding. In particular we may mimic distress when another person is exhibiting that emotion; it is basically an expression of sympathy to that person.

Of all the facial expressions we are capable of transmitting, it is accepted that the one that needs to be encouraged is the *smile*. Happiness is the only *positive* emotion we can show through the face. What are we trying to convey in most of our interpersonal dealings with other people, a negative or a positive state? Do we feel better when we're in a negative state or a positive state? You know how it is. You're in a good mood and you come across somebody who (for no valid reason) is miserable and unsmiling. Doesn't it take away some of your joy? There seems to be only one answer: *smile*. It will cost you nothing, and will leave behind you a trail of goodwill.

You can exhibit a beaming smile when you're actually feeling quite morose. But what is difficult to control are our gestures and our tone of voice (which we shall look at later).

Eye contact is a particularly effective non-verbal means of establishing good interpersonal communication. When we look at someone, they are aware that they have our attention. It then directs the course of the interchange, so its importance cannot be overstressed. We tend to use eye contact for feedback purposes, to make the speaker aware that we are listening to them. We in turn need a signal that they know we are listening to them.

We tend to use eye contact automatically and unconsciously, and perhaps not enough in many work instances. Think about yourself in your work life. How much of it do you do? Think about your work colleagues. How do they compare to you? We tend to engage in more eye contact when we're in a listening situation. A speaker should look at his audience – of one or a hundred – to obtain feedback. If you don't look, you won't know if they're still with you, whether they understand what you're saying, whether you're proceeding too rapidly for comprehension, and of course whether they agree. Lack of eye contact gives the impression that you are talking *at* people instead of *to* them.

Increasing eye contact generally has a positive effect. It can show that you're attentive, that you like somebody and that you're sincere; it can initiate a communication between two people and maintain the interchange once a dialogue has started; it can be a tremendous 'influencer' when trying to persuade somebody to buy your point of view or product; and, on the basis that we fix and maintain eye contact with somebody we're attracted to, it's good for romance!

When most people talk of body language, it is the use of gestures which provide added meaning that they are referring to. Research by psychologists over the years has shown that these gestures can typically be split into five categories:

1 *Emblems*: particular movement(s) used instead of words.
2 *Illustrators*: movement(s) used along with speech.
3 *Regulators*: movements related to our function of speaking or listening, indicating our intentions.

4 *Adaptors*: movements (such as drumming the fingers, pulling hair or fiddling with an item of jewellery) that indicate emotions.
5 *Affect displays*: clearer signals that reveal emotion (such as facial expressions).

If we're to make any sense of body language, *it is essential that we don't take a gesture on its own*, regardless of other gestures or the particular situation, and try to make an analysis. We should use the clues provided by a number of the speaker's gestures – known as 'cluster gestures' – together with their verbal expressions. For example, in the meeting between the business colleagues above, Caine's staring at his shoe, looking at his watch, tapping his foot, picking fluff from his clothes, and lack of real eye contact were a meaningful gesture cluster taken in conjunction with his unconvincing verbalisations.

The inconsistencies that occur between cues from different channels are termed *interchannel discrepancies* by psychologists.

If we receive from two separate channels of communication (i.e. verbal and non-verbal) a conflicting message, the receiver will more likely believe the message that is harder to fake. This is usually the non-verbal message. Therefore, the non-verbal communication will be accepted as true, rather than the verbal one.

It is essential, if you want to successfully communicate the right message to your audience, that verbal and non-verbal messages are 'congruent'. The two mustn't be at odds with each other. Congruence and gesture clusters provide us with the means to accurately interpret body language.

Can you remember a time when you were sitting outside the interviewer's office acting calm and composed, smiling at the secretary, Rosa Klebb, as she brings you a coffee, sardonic smile on her face? ('What does she know that I don't? Has somebody else already been given the job?')

You place the coffee cup on the table, sit up straight, adjust your tie, cross your legs, uncross them, cross them again, fiddle with your watchstrap, smooth your hair, uncross your legs. By the time your prospective interrogator comes out to greet you – 'We've been ex-pec-ting you, Mees-ter Bond' – you're a nervous wreck!

The term 'leakage' is used in body language terms to denote how the message you give someone verbally is invalidated by the truth leaking out visually (commonly from the lower half of the body). In other words, true emotions leak out even when a person tries to conceal them.

Avoiding negative body language signals

When we study body language and its effects, the most important thing to remember is that regardless of what a particular gesture means to you, *it's how the receiver perceives it that's important*.

Various irritating body signals are commonly given out to others:

Crossed arms

There are a few variations to the arm-cross over the chest, but the message is the same. Usually it's a defensive stance; you'll see it on tube trains, in coffee bars, in lifts. In a one-to-one or a meeting situation, you'll see it when the person disagrees with you. It should alert you to the fact that, unless you take action, you might as well give up.

The essential point here is that the 'leakage' signal can give you an opportunity to change tack before the other person has had a chance to put their feelings into words – before it's too late. It happens in family arguments, sales presentations, seminars, meetings with the boss, and at interviews. One subtle method of getting the other person away from this 'closed' body position is to hand them something to look at.

*Anne (noticing that her nephew John has gone into the fold-
    ed-arms position after being ticked off – unfairly in his eyes
    – for once again forgetting her birthday; he'd had exams*

and was preoccupied): 'I kept this interesting cutting from last week's paper for Tanya about a memory system that has helped people in exams. Now, where did I put it? Oh, here it is. Have a look, John.' *(Passes paper to John.)*

John: *(unfolding his tight arm-cross):* 'Yeah. Right. Thanks.'

Interviewee: 'Well, I don't really care for travelling that much, to be frank. I find it so disruptive when you get back from work trips. It takes me a while to readjust to life.'

Interviewer: 'So, if we picked up a client account with international offices, it's not an account that we could consider you for?' *(Folds his arms and leans back. He's losing interest in this applicant, who at first seemed promising. True, the advertisement hadn't mentioned the need for overseas travel, but there was the chance that it might be necessary in the future.)*

Interviewee (reading the body language and realising he'd perhaps been a bit too 'frank'): 'Oh, of course if a client account necessitated work with their overseas offices, it would be a challenge to work within the whole international corporate structure. It's not something I would want to pass up – far from it.'

Having verbally tried to allay the interviewer's concerns, the interviewee now wants to create an *open* body position on the other side of the desk, so he says: 'Could I just show you this artwork from . . . ?'

Interviewer: 'Sure.' *(Reaches over to accept it.)*

Back to open body position!

Sitting positions

We can often deduce a person's mind-set from the way they are sitting:

1 Leg-crossing can accompany the folded arms position or be displayed on its own. It isn't necessarily a negative position. You have to look for the clusters. Women were often told from an early age that it was the correct way to sit. If

accompanied by folded arms it can be a negative/defensive signal. If you're trying to make a point to somebody or sell a product, for example, it's difficult to look enthusiastic with your arms folded and/or legs crossed. And it's not very convincing for the other person. An open position is necessary.

2 When someone remains slouched in a chair when you walk in, rather than getting up to greet you, the impression given is not favourable. Some interviewers are guilty of doing this. You may have come across this at work when going to see your boss. It doesn't make you feel good. It can be used to make you feel inferior or that you're a time-waster.

3 Do you sometimes sit with both hands behind your head? (This is common with men but not with women.) You may do it unconsciously, because you happen to be feeling good and everything's going your way. But, as was stressed earlier on in the chapter, it's the effect that your body language has on *other* people that you need to be aware of. This gesture is often used by people who are feeling superior or confident (for example, a manager who is feeling great because he's telling the person whom he's been dying to get rid of that his employment is terminated!), but it can be extremely offensive or irritating to the onlooker.

Open hand and body gestures are generally used to convey a positive, friendly attitude to the speaker. If you're trying to influence somebody to agree to a course of action or persuade them of something, use open gestures: time and time again they have been shown to be the most effective.

4 Another sitting gesture is possibly one that you've used in trying to get away from an aunt or grandparent. You know the one I mean: where you either grip the chair as if to go, or lean forward with your hands on your knees. But you never quite make it because either another anecdote comes out or another home-made custard tart is offered!

In business this is a valuable pointer to your next move. The other person is satisfied and is waiting for you to move on to the next step, or wants to end the session (they may have another meeting or other things to do). If there is a negative reason, you will have picked this up by observing other cluster leaks. It would pay you to make the first move and initiate the ending of the meeting with whatever follow-up is necessary. It can cause frustration if a person signals to you to end the encounter and you don't pick it up, or take heed. They then have to start the ritual all over again.

5 Sitting perched on the edge of your chair creates a nervous impression. It can indicate to the other person that you don't really want to be there. It could be because you are nervous yourself or that you haven't really got the time or perhaps the inclination. Either way it doesn't create a favourable impression.

Other gestures

There are a whole host of other body signals that can be mis-interpreted (or interpreted correctly!): you'll see people who, while apparently paying attention to you, are tapping their feet, peering over their glasses, touching their nose, rubbing their eyes or ears, touching their mouth, clenching their hands, drumming their fingertips, blinking a lot, playing with their hair, playing with jewellery or a watch, rocking in their chair, playing with pens, or looking at their fingernails excessively. These are just a few mannerisms that could be giving out negative vibes. Watch out for them, and check your own body language.

Spatial relationships

Posture can be an indicator of the intensity of a person's emotions when part of a cluster. If someone changes subject to a confidential topic, they may alter their body posiition to bring the other person closer. People tend to lean forward, towards each other, when there is a degree of respect or liking.

An important aspect of body language analysis is the

concept of *spatial relationships*, in other words your personal space preferences, which dictate the distance from people at which you are comfortable. The closer the proximity, the more intimate that relationship will tend to be. Psychologists have identified four distinct zones:

1 *The intimate*. This, the first zone, extends up to about 18 inches from the body. It will include close friends, spouse and family.
2 *The personal*. Roughly split into two sub-zones of (a) 18 inches–30 inches, which can include spouse and close friends and (b) 30 inches–48 inches, which is quite close proximity, found when conversing with people at a party, for example.
3 *The social*. From 4 feet to 12 feet, the distance between people who do not know each other that well. It could apply to a seminar situation or a distance from someone higher in the hierarchy at work.
4 *The public*. Upwards of 12 feet. A comfortable distance for being with strangers. If you're speaking at a meeting this is the zone you would feel comfortable with, as far as distance from your audience is concerned.

It appears that most of us are quite happy to engage in conversations within the personal zone. In business or other formal circumstances, the social zone seems to be used. We all have our own personal space 'bubble' around us which follows us around. It is as well to remember this when interacting with new acquaintances.

An understanding of the communication of bodily movements used when people interact with each other – the science of 'kinesics', as it is known – is an important one.

Hopefully, as well as observing other people's non-verbal behaviour, you'll have realised that you should always be saying to yourself: 'What is the impression I am sending with my body language? *And is that what I want?*'

6

Make your memory pay

All knowledge is but remembrance.
Plato

A poor memory threatens everything in life: personal relationships, business contacts, income, health – the list is endless. Most of what we say is founded on something that has happened, something that we did or that somebody else did. So, if your recall of your own valuable experiences, or others' words of wisdom is that bit better than the average person's, you're bound to come out on top. When people are questioned about the attributes they would like that they don't believe they possess, a good memory is always near the top of the list.

The problem is that a lot of people have very average memories and many others have very bad ones. If you can break from this mould, you're in a very powerful position. In business and personal life, the confidence that comes from a good power of recall is valuable beyond measure. And we all have it within us to improve our memories and therefore our lives.

Let's take a quick look at the way in which cognitive psychologists like to compare the human mind to a computer, and memory to an information-processing system. In today's IT world, the analogy affords a useful way to see how 'breakdown' can occur in the system. The PC receives input from the keyboard: it converts the symbols to a numeric code; the information is saved on the disk; data is retrieved from your disk either by displaying it on the computer screen or printing it out. If there's a breakdown in the system, or there's not enough disk space, or if you delete the file, you'll find that the information's been 'forgotten', as you're unable to access the information.

Following on from this, researchers in the field of memory have attempted to look at the way any information that we receive is processed mentally, in the information-processing system. In this context, a stimulus that registers in our sensory system will only be remembered if it (a) draws attention, which brings it into consciousness; (b) it becomes encoded in the brain and stored; and (c) it is retrieved for use at some later stage.

Three types of memory thus become identified: sensory, short-term and long-term.

Sensory memory

This refers to things that are stored for a very brief period of time, ranging from a fraction of a second to perhaps three seconds. This form of memory is difficult to distinguish from the act of perception. For example, it would contain an image of something just glimpsed or a fleeting sound that was just heard. The sensations that do not draw attention simply disappear, as no analysis is performed on the information; those sensations that are 'noticed' are transferred to the next form of memory, short-term memory.

Short-term memory

This is a very interesting side of memory cognition. The key to it is *attention*. Short-term memory has a limited storage facility in terms of the number of items it can store and in duration. In other words, in the *amount* of information and how long it can store it.

Research into how many items a person can store with correct recall has shown a figure of seven (plus or minus two), whether they be numbers, names, letters or words. Short-term memory has its limits, and rightly so. Going back to the computer and information-processing model, it is like removing old and unwanted files from your disk. Can you imagine the situation if you couldn't clear unwanted items from your short-term memory? Your mind would contain trivia such as your lottery numbers of three weeks ago, unwanted telephone numbers, every sensation that you'd ever experienced.

Recall usually relies on *repetition* and *rehearsal*, or the information can just disappear as quickly as it entered your consciousness. For example, you may hear a telephone number on the radio ('Call for the free factsheet on 0634 56329'), dash to the phone (there's no pen handy, of course!), and as you get to the fifth digit you have to hang up because the rest of the number has gone from your head. Or you're at a party and, while you're chatting to somebody you met twenty minutes ago, your husband comes over; as you introduce him to your new acquaintance you can't remember her name.

The repetition method (or 'maintenance rehearsal' as a leading pioneer in memory research termed it) of repeating the information silently (or aloud if circumstances allow it) would have helped in both these instances. 'Rehearsal' is used to 'maintain' the information in the short-term memory indefinitely.

Long-term memory

You can rehearse information in your short-term memory until it eventually becomes stored in your long-term memory. This contains information that is thought about in a more meaningful and deeper way and associated with other knowledge that is already stored in the long-term memory ('elaborative rehearsal'). Unlike short-term memory, long-term memory has no known limits. Information stored here does not become lost if it isn't retrieved or rehearsed. It can be called up as needed.

An important aspect of elaborative rehearsal in long-term memory is the linking of new information to the self. The self, in other words, can be used as a memory aid. You're *relating information to what you already know – forming associations*. You elaborate on new information by recollecting information that you already have stored in your long-term memory.

If we process any new information as relevant to our own experiences, we consider the information in a deeper fashion and our recall is vastly improved. If you met someone at a party who had the same birthday as you – month, date and year – wouldn't you be more likely remember them and their name, than someone whom you perhaps found equally interesting at the party? If a prospective client went to the same university as you, there's a good chance you might remember that, even if you didn't see them again for a few years and you bumped into them later. True, you might have remembered the face – with long-term memory certain types of data, such as people's faces, are encoded without any conscious effort – but you may also know their name, where you met them, and what university they graduated from. (If the other person's memory is poor or average, they'll be astounded that you remembered which university they attended – but how you did it is your secret!)

Coding

Information is stored in two fashions or 'codes'. These have important implications in terms of improving our memories. Firstly, there is *semantic coding*. Any verbal communication is processed in terms of the *meaning* of the communication as a whole, not the specific words that made up the message. For example:

John (to his colleague, Janice): 'So I had to tell Mrs Hughes that if we don't get the postroom to speed up delivery to individual departments, she'll have to hire somebody to come in at 7 am to do a preliminary sort, to make things quicker for the boys when they get in at 8 pm.'

Janice (recounting John's conversation later on): 'John's going to get somebody in at seven if things don't improve. He's cleared it with his boss.'

Sally: 'Look, Dad. If I don't get a mobile phone, then if the train's late or breaks down, I'm going to find it difficult letting you know when to pick me up from the station. Those telephone boxes never work . . . Susan's mum gave her and Alice one as presents last month.'

Dad (talking to his wife that evening): 'Yes, she says it's handy if the trains are delayed or whatever, for letting us know.

Her friend Susan and her sister got them as presents for Christmas or something. I don't think we can get out of it.'

So it's the *semantic construction* that is stored, with a fair dose of 'reading between the lines' so that we recall not just what we thought we heard but also what was *implied* during part of the message. In the second example above, Dad said his daughter's friend had got one for Christmas; she just mentioned 'presents'.

Most verbal information is stored in our long-term memory in a semantic way. Visual inputs and many other items of information are more likely stored as *visual images*. Using imagery to remember things, as research constantly shows, is highly effective. Forming an image of words and relating them in an interactive way with something else that needs to be remembered is a common technique that people use.

The key is to make it *memorable*. Say you had to remember to (1) post a letter and (2) pick up your dry cleaning on the way to taking your car in to the garage for a service (3) and (4) ask the mechanic for the umbrella you left there when you dashed in a few days earlier, you might form a mental image covering all four intended actions, an interactive one that relates all four activities. And because it's in your imagination it can be as bizarre as you like.

Your first image might be a post box (1); then an image of you wearing a dry-cleaned suit with the plastic covers still on it (2); then a scene with your car in the garage forecourt (3) with your umbrella hooked over the steering-wheel like one of those security devices (4). All of these images could be connected in your mind by a picture of you sitting in the driving seat of your car wearing a suit with the dry cleaning cover on it; in front of you, your steering-wheel is 'locked' with your umbrella, and there is a postbox perched on the roof of your car! Just *one* image now. Rehearse it in your mind a few times (don't tell anybody about it!) and after it has enabled you to carry out the functions, jettison it from your memory. Mission accomplished.

On a practical, everyday level it is probably now clear that most problems relating to a person's poor or average recall relates to what happens when they're encoding information. Encoding means actually getting this material into memory. Psychologists continually prove that the process of retrieval is considerably enhanced by frequent rehearsal.

Some information that was unrehearsed gets encoded and stored into the memory with very little attention or effort. This is known as *automatic processing*. But, as we have seen, most material cannot successfully be encoded unless attention is paid to it.

How we encode the information directly affects our chances of *remembering* it. Giving the information some *personal meaning* reduces the likelihood that we will forget it.

Remembering names

You've said it to yourself a thousand times: 'I remember the face, but I can't remember the name.' Remembering names appears to be the biggest problem for most people, especially in the working world. And yet the name is the most important piece of information that we need to know about an individual. If you forget somebody's name you're aiming a knockdown shot at the ego – and it's bull's-eye. Although it might not be made obvious, you've lost a few points immediately. Your *faux pas* may only register in the other person's subconscious, but it is still significant.

In most cases it's not that you actually forget a name. You probably never picked it up in the first place, because you failed to *hear* it properly and did nothing to rectify this. This could be because:

1 It is an interest problem: you just weren't interested enough to fully catch the person's name and 'store' it.
2 You were distracted at the time of the introduction because your mind was elsewhere.

Whatever the reason, it's *not good enough*. Remembering names is such a potent social skill or persuasion tool that, if you do nothing else, you must make the effort to improve in this area.

When you use somebody's name, you find that you receive more attention; it's human nature. Whatever 'two-timing' in terms of straying thoughts, may be going on in our head, at the mention of our name our ears prick up.

You'll notice this when you're out shopping, or at your bank or building society, or eating in a restaurant. The widespread use of credit cards, cheques and loyalty cards has led to organisations referring to people by name, to add a personal touch. Hotels and airline check-in desks have been doing this for years, of course:

'Enjoy your meal, Miss . . .'

'How would you like your money, Mr . . . ?'

'Any problems with the toaster Mr . . . , please bring it back to us.'

'I hope the room's OK for you Miss . . . Just call down to reception if you'd like to change.'

'Have a good flight, Mr . . .'

They've realised the success of such a basic appeal to vanity. It's a caressing of the ego that works wonders. It's just a simple gesture – but it can have a great effect. Because people like to be recognised. They go back to places where people know them.

Canny people in any business make a point of committing names to memory – if not their own, then on the hard disk of their computer!

There is no better way of selling yourself to someone than being *interested* enough to remember their name. Have you noticed in your love life how it works wonders? When you're returning something faulty to a store and you've remembered the name of the person that served you? (OK – you found it on the bill – I won't tell!) When you're in a business meeting with more than one person and you remember the names of the 'least important' members of the meeting? (Hey, they can influence too, you know.) Business has been won or lost because a person's name was remembered or forgotten.

You can improve yourself mentally, just as you can improve your physique from workouts in the gym. Everyone has the ability. Become your own personal trainer. Conditioning the mind through mental jogging can help develop a more effective memory for names.

Interest is flattering

If you remember something about a person, they feel flattered; you're appealing to their ego:

'You were going to see *Cats* the last time I saw you. How was it?'

'You told me last time that the Upper Class service on Virgin was impressive. Taking your word for it, I'm flying next week.'

'When we spoke in March, you'd just exchanged contracts on your house. Have you moved in yet?'

'You were having problems with the contractors over your new offices the last time we met. Sorted out now?'

To make way for valuable information to be stored in our memory, as we observed earlier on in the chapter, it's necessary to 'de-clutter' it. You have to relegate useless information to the 'recycle bin'. (Thank you for the imagery, Bill Gates!) There are people who can give you the FA Cup results since 1964 but can't remember their car number plate. They can recite the last ten minutes of *Gone With the Wind* but wouldn't have a hope of remembering their PIN Number. A readjustment is needed.

Remember, the first essential is a conscious effort to be *interested*. One person's lack of knowledge about another results from no effort being made to take an interest. Even in a lot of friendships, empathy and understanding can sadly be a one-way affair. Some people are so superficial in their dealings with others that the conversation often goes something like this:

'How's things, Mark?'

'Well, business isn't that good at the moment. And I had a burglary last week . . .'

'Good, good . . . I wanted to ask if you might . . .'

How can you possibly remember things if you don't programme your mind to register what the other person is saying? It's selfishness, really. If you want something from another person – friendship, a job, a sale, help, money, sympathy – you've got to be interested enough to remember things connected with them. It allows you to establish a productive two-way relationship.

The simplest way to improve memory is by *association*. You may come across people with whom you have something in common; this ought to help you to remember facts about them. It could be many things: age, birthplace, love of a sport, car, a holiday, a name, a whole host of possible things. This common factor can easily trigger a memory association. And since the other person's memory isn't that good, they will have forgotten they ever told you about their new car, holiday, recent accident, etc. As a result, when you say: 'How's your Ferrari running?' or 'Played any tennis lately?' or 'How was Sardinia?' or 'Is your husband better?' they can't help but be surprised – and *impressed*. 'How did you know . . . ?'

A few years ago I dealt with a prospective client whose young daughter, it turned out, shared a birthday that was the same as my own. He happened to mention that I shouldn't call him on such and such a day as he wouldn't be in the office: it was his daughter's birthday and he was taking her out. I mentioned to him that it was also *my* birthday.

A couple of years later, I met him at the same exhibition at the same time of year. I said to him: 'How are you celebrating your daughter's birthday on Thursday?'

He nearly collapsed! He might just have accepted that somebody could have found out *his* birthday, but not his six-year-old daughter's! Of course, he didn't remember that I shared the same birthday (which would explain my 'good memory'). He went through all the possible explanations as to how I could know this – I was having an affair with his wife; I had found out from a lost diary of his (even though he hadn't lost a diary!) – but he couldn't get it. I left him guessing. You see, most people have poor memories.

The prerequisite to effective recall is always *interest*. I associated a fact that I forced myself to be interested in with something that I already had stored in my long-term memory – my own birthday.

Making associations

If you were shown 150 photographs of celebrities from the entertainment world and public life, the chances are that you might be able to name upwards of 130. And yet you probably have not met even one of these people.

You recognised their faces and you remembered their names. The reason is that you're interested in retaining the name, and used (unconsciously) whatever associations you needed to remember the name. If you were shown a photograph of the actress Elizabeth Taylor in the role of Cleopatra, it's probably Cleopatra that makes you remember her name (or possibly the other way round).

The secret of remembering names lies with the individual. It's back to your own imagination again. Certain names you will remember without difficulty:

1 Those of people who are important in your daily life. You'll naturally remember the names of your relatives, friends, work colleagues, business clients, your doctor, your bank manager, etc.
2 Those of people who have had a great influence on your life. For example, your old headteacher; the person who interviewed you for your first job; the person who handed you the Lottery cheque for £1.4 million; the driving examiner who enabled you to tear up your L-plates when you passed your driving test at the third attempt.

But what about the people we come across whose names we would *like* to remember, socially or perhaps during a business meeting? The problem's the same, although it's more crucial in a formal business setting.

Many names, at least surnames, can be significant to us. We can equate them with something and paint word pictures. Names such as Harper, Walker and Shepherd – they're easy. With names like Longman, Royle and Silver an association could easily be formed.

Now, we must get one thing straight: your imagination belongs to *you*. When I've been giving presentations relating to memory techniques, people have come up to me in the coffee breaks and said that they find it embarrassing to make up silly associations in their heads. I can understand the concern. But until we enter the *Star Trek* age, where people can look into your mind, you're safe!

What goes on in the top floor of your anatomy is your affair. If you devise daft methods of remembering names, and it helps you in your life, *go ahead*.

Let's take the examples above: for Harper you could picture a person playing a harp; Walker: perhaps visualise a person with a rucksack; Shepherd: sheep in his arms; Longman picture the person as a circus l-o-n-g man; Royle: imagine the person with a crown on his head; Silver: imagine the person with a black patch over one eye. The possibilities are endless, and begin and end with you.

If these visual pictures don't prompt your memory, nothing will. Picture individuals in this way and make a point of registering the pictures in your mind. Then, when you look at these people, it will be to the accompaniment of your finely tuned imagination.

While they're frantically trying to remember your name, you'll be reeling off theirs; it will trip off the tongue. They won't know how you do it (which may be just as well!).

But *you* know how. It's magic. The magic of memory.

Introductions

Often, as we discussed earlier, it's not a case of forgetting a name. It's rather that it simply didn't register in the first place.

This is nothing more than laziness or disinterest. Or nerves. Nerves? Why nerves?

It seems that when we meet people for the first time, the momentary shock to the system diverts us from our normal listening process. We're so aware of what we're going to say, what we look like, and the impression we are giving, that we miss the name when it's announced. So it's not that we've forgotten the name a few seconds later. It's more likely that we just didn't hear it. But the other person doesn't always know that. And quite often they won't give you the benefit of the doubt. Especially if they've heard and remembered *your* name!

If you don't catch somebody's name at the outset (or if it simply isn't given), the few seconds of handshake (if that's the formal type of situation you're in) afford ample opportunity to ask the other person to *repeat* it. There is a general reluctance, almost embarrassment about doing this, for fear of seeming rude. On the contrary, it demonstrates politeness. Our name is the most personal thing we possess – it's unique to us. It forms a big part in the psychology of the 'self'. Consequently, people are often more responsive to those who use it.

Two people are introduced to each other by a third party. They shake hands.

'Hello. I'm Sue Madsen.'

'Pleased to meet you. John Watkins.'

It sounds straightforward, but one or the other or both of these people are capable of missing the name because of the concern or worry of *what to say next*. As they are being introduced, their minds are simultaneously working on the next sentence. The name can be blotted out. It's not a memory problem in this case; it's a *hearing* problem.

Think back to a party you've been to. On arrival, a bottle of *Cabernet Sauvignon* in hand, you are confronted with a roomful of faces. You're introduced to a string of people. One by one, names are reeled off: 'Richard – this is Eileen, Simon, Sheila, Paul, Tom, Andrew, Jacqueline . . .'

At the same time you are trying to take in many other aspects of the scene – the decor, the people in the background, the music, how much wine there is left, and anything else that catches your eye.

These distractions, combined with your own self-consciousness at meeting all these new people, mean that you probably catch only one or two names, if that. And even then you don't always attach the right name to the right face. It's not so bad for the people you're being introduced to. They have only one name to remember at the time – yours. Also, they have already established their territory, so they're more relaxed. It's much easier to remember things when you're relaxed.

You probably end up gravitating initially towards the two people whose names you happened to pick up. Just your luck – the two biggest bores, those awful types who have taken out their own appendix or done their own conveyancing when selling their house!

Rule 1: *Make sure that you hear the name.*

Imagine that you arrive at the office of a client, Mr Good, for a meeting with him and three other members of his division, including his boss, the managing director, Mr King.

As you enter the boardroom, your contact Mr Good introduces you to his three colleagues: 'Nice to see you again. I'd like to introduce you to Simon King our managing director, Jason Templar from publicity, and Annette Barnes from information technology.'

You fail to hear Mr King's name at all. As you shift your briefcase uneasily from your right to your left hand, in readiness to shake his hand, you mutter: 'Er . . . How d'you do.' You manage to catch the names Templar and Barnes: 'How do you do. Mr Templar, Miss Barnes.'

You're shown to a seat and the discussion starts. Mr Good had mentioned on a previous occassion that his boss, Mr King, was the one with the ultimate authority to give a go-ahead, he was the decision-maker. Nothing could be agreed, he'd said, unless the managing director went along with it. But his boss was apparently a reasonable man – a 'people person' – who liked to know he was dealing with somebody with integrity and empathy, somebody he could trust. Hence the group meeting in which he wanted to be present.

Since you can't remember his (Mr King's) name, you find yourself addressing Mr Templar, whose name you did catch, and also your original contact, Mr Good. (Your short-term memory registered the name Templar because it's also the name of the street where you live; that, plus rehearsal and good mental imagery, meant that remembering his name was no problem throughout the meeting.) Mr Good happens to be the least influential member of the group as far as this project is concerned. Yet you end up directing most of your points and questions to him. Why? Because you know his name and find yourself automatically veering towards him.

Mr King and Miss Barnes are not given as much attention. Yet *they* are the two people with the power to agree to the proposal. It is with them that you should have been trying hard to establish a level of empathy and rapport.

This scenario occurs every day in business meetings (and socially). It does not promote effective communication. But it's so easy to avoid. And what positive results are achieved by doing so!

It's so simple. At the start, the obvious statement 'I'm sorry, I didn't catch your name' would have been the solution. But most people don't do it. Why?

People seem to assume that the attitude of the other person is: 'Either you get my name the first time, or forget it.' As though it's an unforgiveable *faux pas*. As though the person who has dared to ask for the name to be repeated should be written off as slow, stupid, unprofessional, or all three.

Don't ever feel embarrassed about admitting that you didn't hear a name. There's a two-fold advantage to this:

1 You are actually sure of the name.
2 As a psychological plus, you make the person you are meeting *feel more important*. You've shown that you consider knowing their name worthwhile.

Rule 2: If you hear a name, make sure you put it to the right face.

If you have ever got people's names crossed during a meeting or in a social situation, it's probably something you won't want to repeat. The embarrassment can be so great that if you are ever in any doubt it is often better to use no name at all. And this will definitely reduce your effectiveness as a communicator whose aim is to create rapport with a particular set of individuals. Certainly, calling the person by the wrong name is infinitely worse than not remembering the name at all.

Mnemonics

A useful tip for matching names to faces of people at a group meeting is to take the first letters of their names and line them up in your mind (according to the seating) to form a word (if you're lucky) or abbreviation. This is termed '*mnemonics*' and is a useful technique for improving memory.

Take, for example, the initials of the people at the meeting described above: Mr K, Mr T and Miss B. Assuming they are safely seated so you know where they are, you can repeat in your mind 'KTB, KTB' a few times to ensure that you know exactly who is who. Try it the next time you're in this kind of situation; it's a simple but effective aid.

The importance of names

If you want to test how much importance you subconsciously attach to names in a work situation, catch yourself when you're at a conference, exhibition, seminar, etc. Visitors and delegates are probably wearing the obligatory plastic lapel name badges. You spot a familiar face but can't remember the name. That may deter you in the first instance from actually going up to her for a chat. If you do, you probably end up not concentrating on the conversation because intermittently (and subtly – or so you think!) you're trying to sneak a look at the name on the badge.

She's remembered *your* name and *your* company. That's put even more stress on you. You feel terribly embarrassed. You've been so intent on trying to read her name badge – but the light's been shining on the plastic and you couldn't see – that you've missed most of what she's said. She asks you a question related to the discussion. You're at a loss because you haven't been listening. This looks like lack of interest. She thinks you're a waste of time and moves off, politely, at the earliest opportunity.

You still didn't get her name. And now she's got the wrong impression about you, on top of everything else.

Sometimes it pays to ask somebody else, discreetly, the name of the person concerned: 'My memory's going. Who's that over there?' If you don't know the person that well, and it's quite acceptable that it has slipped your mind (i.e., it wouldn't cause offence), then 'Sorry, your name's escaped me' – or the equivalent – is permissible. Sometimes, through good fortune, the person in question, if in a group, will automatically shake hands with a new arrival and identify himself. That solves your problem.

A true story

The recognition factor is a strong streak running through all of us. As we have seen, to be recognised is a measure of self-esteem; it gives people an inner satisfaction. 'People know me.' The ego's hunger for recognition gives you an opportunity to gain points when you remember another person's name.

A marketing manager is going to the United States for a meeting with prospective clients arranged by the local advertising agency executive.

When he arrives in the US, the marketing manager, Thomas Hart, telephones the agency man, Chuck Madsen, to find out the arrangements for the meeting. His call is greeted by a voicemail message asking him to leave a message. He leaves this message: 'Hello, Chuck. It's Thomas Hart from London. I'm here in San Francisco now and I'm at Hotel . . .'

The next day he has a call from Chuck: 'Tom! How ya doin'? It's Chuck Madsen here. Good to talk to you . . . Meeting's fixed for tomorrow at ten-thirty. Pick you up at about ten. Is that OK?'

'Fine. I'll be ready.'

The following day they meet as arranged and proceed to the client's offices. On their arrival, two men greet them. Chuck says: 'Bill, Pete, I'd like to introduce you to our friend from London – Thomas Clark.'

What should Tom do now. Does he say, 'Actually it's Tom H-a-r-t' and embarrass Chuck, who fixed up the meeting?

'Good to meet you, Mr Clark. Hope you didn't bring any fog over from London. We've enough of our own. I've seen those Jack the Ripper movies!' They both shake hands with him. 'Hey, can we call you Tom?' ('Please,' he thinks. 'Anything but Clark!')

Tom's performance during the meeting is completely stilted. Naturally enough, he doesn't feel comfortable with his new-found identity. Of course he is eventually given a business card by each of his new acquaintances. He automatically reaches to hand out his own, but quickly retracts. This is now completely out of the question.

He blames Chuck. He accepts the difficulties of hearing a name accurately over the phone, especially from a voicemail message, but he expected Chuck to have known his correct name before he arrived, or double-checked it, if he'd forgotten. Tom can't concentrate now, and is unable to give his best performance. It's fine that they're calling him Tom, during the meeting, but what about further contact if a business relationship develops. Yes he should have corrected the name at first but for a silly reason – saving Chuck from losing face – he didn't.

After the uninspired meeting, full of bonhomie, but not much substance, Tom leaves the office with Chuck. He considers telling him about the problem. But he doesn't want to make him feel a fool, even now. With any luck, nothing further will progress, as they're seeing a number of other companies for the project, he thinks. So he'll probably never see these people again. Fortunately, he receives no calls at the hotel over the next two days, right up to the time he leaves for London.

Two years later he is speaking to one of his bosses, who has just returned from the West Coast of the US.

'I met a guy called Chuck Madsen at the seminar last week,' he remarks. 'Apparently you met him two, three years ago. Spoke very highly of you – except he was a bit puzzled about something.'

'Oh, what?'

'I told him he must be mistaken. He said that when you were over there you went round calling yourself Clark not Hart!'

Let's try and analyse what went wrong two years earlier:

1 Chuck simply may not have listened properly; or
2 He may have just forgotten the name; or
3 The telephone was to blame for blurring Tom's message.

In any case, to be absolutely sure, Chuck should have checked with hotel reception, or have clarified it with Tom Hart when they first met; perfectly in order in such circumstances.

Instead, all parties lost out:

1 Chuck Madsen could have enhanced his reputation by introducing his clients to somebody with the means of making their campaigns more successful in Europe. He would have had some reflected glory (and a large fee), and it would have strengthened the bond between advertising agency and client.
2 The prospective clients in the US lost out on a UK connection that would have benefited them.
3 Tom Hart missed out on lucrative and prestigious business for which he had spent a lot of time preparing. And he felt embarrassed about contacting Chuck again. It wasn't the sort of impression he really wanted to create at all.

It could be argued that it was partly Tom's fault. When he first met Chuck he could have introduced himself again just to make sure. Or he could, as a matter of courtesy, have handed over his business card. The chances are, none of this would have occurred. If the voicemail message had been responsible for the mistake, it would have been rectified as soon as the two men met at the hotel.

Business cards can be trumps

As we've seen, in the sometimes extremely formal settings of work encounters, getting names right can be crucial. Fortunately, we're sometimes helped with the common currency of the world of work: the business card. These are almost universal ('Could I have your card?' 'Here's my card'), yet there are some people who take great delight in not having them, precisely because they are in such common use.

But there's no question that a card can be useful for a number of reasons:

1 It establishes the image of you or your company.
2 It supplies your name and status at the outset.
3 It can provide an interesting opener when you meet some-one, and establishes initial ice-breaking conversation.
4 From the memory aspect, it solves your immediate short-term memory challenge, as you have the card in front of you in case you forget the person's name in the course of your conversation.

People vary in their preferences about *when* to hand over a business card. Offering your own card at the beginning of a meeting generally helps the other person to remember your name and to evaluate your status. They will usually reciprocate, allowing you to confirm or evaluate their posi-tion too. But some people hand over their cards at the end of a meeting.

If you think you'll have trouble remembering the person's name or are unsure of it, then be sure to exchange cards at the start, when you arrive. Then keep theirs in view so that you can refer to it. They are probably doing the same with yours. It's on the desk in front of them, or on the sofa beside them if the seating is informal. They don't want to get your name wrong either.

On a holiday some years ago, I struck up a conversation with a Japanese executive who was swimming up and down the hotel pool. After a few minutes he came out of the water and perched himself by the edge of the pool. He then put his right hand down the front of his swimming trunks and, to the sur-prise – and delight – of the onlookers (who started applauding), produced a waterproof business card, which he handed to me!

Empty promises

A particularly disturbing habit that people exhibit in their everyday lives causes more upsets and misunderstandings than anything else – family feuds, divorces, friends falling out with each other, and fractured business relationships are typical casualties. What causes them? The making of empty promises and statements.

In many cases the person who is promised something that doesn't materialise, forgets anyway, so no harm is done. Relationships continue and business keeps functioning. But in many instances what turned out to be empty words are *forgotten* by the speaker, but *remembered* by the listener. This does not make for harmonious relationships.

Consider this situation:

'Well, I'll see you when I get back from "across the pond".'

'Where are you going exactly?'

'Boston. Then over to Cape Cod and Martha's Vineyard.'

'Lovely. One of those self-drive holidays, is it?'

'Well, I won't be driving in Boston with their traffic. You know the Boston joke – "Shall we walk or have we time to take a taxi?" '

'Yes, quite. You lucky thing. All that lovely maple syrup on those pancakes.'

'You like maple syrup?'

'Yes – used to have it when I worked in Boston and New York for five years or so.'

'I'll bring you some back.'

'Hey, that's kind of you, but there's no need to take the trouble.'

'It'll be no trouble. A pleasure. I'll bring you back one of those large tins. My treat.'

'Well, thanks. My wife will be pleased.'

Typically, our man has *forgotten* this conversation by the time he gets back to the visitors' car park, where he receives a couple of mobile phone messages relating to various problems back at the office. The potential client he has just been to see has a good memory. He even tells his wife that evening that a kind soul would be bringing them back a huge tin of maple syrup from New England.

Five weeks later this 'kind soul' returns from his travels

and makes a follow-up appointment. The conversation goes as follows:

'Well. How was New England?'

Our man is flattered. He feels important. 'What a great guy,' he thinks. 'He remembers I was going on that trip. I can't remember telling him I was going away.' 'Have you ever been there?'

'Er . . . yes. I was over in the Boston and New York area for nearly five years. D'you remember me saying the last time you were here?'

'Oh er . . . er . . . That's right. Of course. You met your wife there, I think.' *(It's obvious from his facial expressions and the rest of his body language that he doesn't remember, or that the recollection is very vague.)*

The disillusioned client is now doubting our man's integrity, he's apparently very superficial. During the rest of the meeting there is no mention of the gift that had been promised so effusively.

The client makes his final evaluation of his visitor as he escorts him to the lift. Apart from feeling slightly angry at the man's lack of self-awareness, he also decides that the man is insincere. His inner feeling is: 'If you can forget this, then if I do business with you you'll forget to give me good customer service after a sale – oh, and you probably also forgot to tell me the drawbacks of your product!'

The moral is: *Woe betide you and your broken promises if the other person has a good memory.* You'll come unstuck.

Come on: get inside the other person's mind. Forgetting a throwaway line – which was quite incidental to the conversation – may seem a trivial thing to you. But it may be significant to the other person involved. What message does it send out about your character and integrity? It's important to remember: people have very different levels of sensitivity.

Casual remarks or promises that may seem unimportant to you may strike a chord with the other person. You're then expected to come up with the goods. If you fail to do so, your true worth as a person is in doubt – and it becomes hard to alter that judgement. In situations like the example given, the client would use such behaviour as a barometer of the other person's trustworthiness.

A poor memory can destroy relationships. But it's an interest problem, so it can be cured. Simply take more interest in whatever is important to the other person.

You must make the effort to pick up people's reactions to what you are saying or doing, in any kind of relationship. More often than not the other party will not convey their real feelings about your sin(s) of omission. Your forgetfulness or thoughtlessness is quite likely to result in a rift. You can lose a friend or you can lose business. And you may not even know why.

Take some everyday situations:

A friend lends you £10 to save you queuing at the bank. *You forget to pay her back*.

Another friend buys your theatre ticket for *Phantom of the Opera*, as you've left your credit card in the car. *You forget to pay her back*.

Your secretary works late to get important reports typed up for you. You promise to buy her a bottle of bubbly for her kindness. *You forget*.

You tell a client that you'll call on Friday with the name of a good physiotherapist for his backache. *You forget*.

Do these situations jog any personal memories? Have you been there? You may have been the perpetrator or on the receiving end. Nobody wants the embarrassment of reminding you that you have not paid your debts or fulfilled your promises. You should make a point of remembering in the first place what you commit yourself to. Otherwise you may eventually find that people have no time for you. They give you the cold shoulder. And you can't think why.

You can't even raid your memory bank to work out the reason – *because it's permanently on overdraft*. You never put anything in!

Remembering figures

In our normal lives we benefit greatly from being able to remember figures, but in a business context it assumes even greater importance – dates, prices, technical details. But there really is no problem even for the person with a so-called 'bad memory'. It's just a question of making a conscious effort, linking them with other figures that already mean something to you, perhaps. The process is shown in Figure 6.

Want proof? I bet you could memorise the calendar for a particular year with no trouble at all. You're sceptical? Really? If somebody walked up to you and said: 'What day

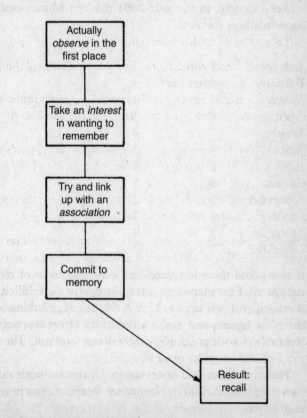

Figure 6 *Steps to attaining a productive memory*

of the week is 25 November next year, 29 April the year
after, 25 May the year after that, 22 August the year after,
2 February the year after, 14 May the year after that?' Well,
I know. You'd tell them to invest in a good ten-year diary.
But suppose you could conjure up the figures in a matter of
seconds? Or, more accurately, your long-term memory could?

You still don't believe it's possible? Have a go. Prove it to
yourself.

As with most memory feats, we're looking for interest
first of all. Be interested enough to commit a few dates to
memory for the year 2001. No. I don't mean 365 days either.
Let's take twelve.

For example, in the year 2001 the first Monday of every
month falls as follows:

		2002	2003	2004
January	1	7	6	5
February	5	4	3	2
March	5	4	3	1
April	2	1	7	5
May	7	6	5	3
June	4	3	2	7
July	2	1	7	5
August	6	5	4	2
September	3	2	1	6
October	1	7	6	4
November	5	4	3	1
December	3	2	1	6

If you know these key dates, it's very easy to work out any
date at all. First memorise just these twelve digits. It's easy to
do this if you pair up, i.e. 15, 52, 74, 26, 31, 53. Now repeat
these six figures and make a conscious effort to remember.
Rehearse in your mind. Repeat them out loud nine times. Got
it?

Now, suppose you're trying to work out what day 25
November is in 2001. November is the eleventh month,
and so the first Monday is the fifth; therefore the 25th is a
Sunday. You see you've done it – in seconds. The 29th April

is another example: the first Monday is the 2nd therefore the 29th is a Sunday. (The corresponding first Monday figures for 2002 to 2004 are also listed above.)

The effect on your audience would be astounding. But isn't it easy to make yourself have a good memory? Looks as though it can be learned, doesn't it? The key is *association*. As illustrated earlier, a good memory is all about association. We associate something we already know (and therefore remember) to provide us with an answer to something else we would *like to know* (and remember). Just by remembering six figures, you have suddenly become, to others, a walking calendar.

Remembering telephone numbers

Association makes it much easier to recall telephone numbers too. It just requires a little deep thinking. There are certain numbers that are etched in our memories – those of relatives, friends, certain business contacts, doctor's surgery, bank, pizza delivery service. But how often are you caught out because you can't remember a number? And so you don't make the call. You'll make it 'later'. Result: end of a relationship; lost business; friction – and more. All because you haven't made a conscious effort to remember a number.

So, again, first be *interested* in memorising the number. Then look for a way of remembering it by relating it to something you already know. Then, when you're trying to recall, your mind will link the two things together.

For example, consider a number: 021-394568. Your imagination provides you with a way of remembering 021 – perhaps how old you were when you graduated – and 3945 happens to be the years when the Second World War started and ended; 68 may be an old flat number of yours as a student. (Would you have tried to make similar associations to these before reading this?) So you've associated a telephone number that you would like to recall at will with facts you already know. You have programmed your mind. (Test: see if you can remember this number in fifty-nine minutes' time.)

Let's take another example: the phone number of a client, Tom Beechwood is 65549. For the person's name, you could imagine a wooden table made of beechwood. Then think of retirement age being 65; 54 might be the year of your birth, and 9 may be your lucky number. Connect these in your mind and see how easy it is. But remember, be interested enough to *want* to remember it. (Test: see if you can remember this in sixty minutes' time.)

(Note: when you've amazed yourself at how competent you've suddenly become at memorising these example numbers, jettison them from your psyche and *substitute* for them two telephone numbers that you've never been able – or bothered – to commit to memory.)

Remembering prices

In a business situation, you may frequently need to remember prices, discounts and other figures relating to various products and services. Of course there is usually a price list of some sort that you may be able to refer to, which means that most business people do not take the time or trouble to commit such figures to memory.

But what about when you need to think on your feet? Being able to remember prices/rates without recourse to written material can often mean the difference between a deal and no deal.

How? Well, it's all tied up with the attention curve, which you'll remember from a previous chapter. (Now *there's* a memory test for you!) Remember the importance of *timing* in a meeting: how an interruption can disturb that emotional high, that fleeting moment that is make or break. Everything that you've said or done before has been leading up to this psychological 'hot spot' of the proceedings. Successful deals are struck at this point. You're asked a question about price, discounts or specifications, and your eye contact is suspended as you look away and ponder over written material. The spell is broken, just as when the television commercial appears as the car is heading towards the edge of the cliff.

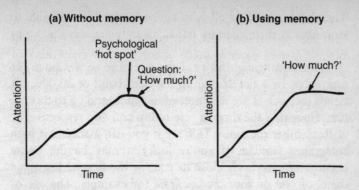

Figure 7 *Maintaining attention by using memory at a crucial moment*

If you were able to memorise prices, for example, you wouldn't have to look away. When the other person asks: 'How much will it be for five thousand units, and what discount would I get if I took fourteen thousand?' instead of breaking the dialogue to rummage through price lists, you can answer immediately. You're giving the other person minimal opportunity to lose concentration, and more importantly, for his emotional state to change.

Most people do not realise how potent the use of memory is at this sensitive stage. *Don't break the dialogue.* Come out with the figures naturally and maintain that eye contact.

The potential attention curves for this situation (see Figure 7) illustrate how efficient use of memory can change the level of the proceedings.

What strategies can be used to remember prices? Your imagination provides the key. It will be different for everybody. But first – as always – make a *conscious decision* to memorise, then look for an association that you can identify with.

Suppose a pricing structure is as follows:

up to 10,000 units	£1.68 per unit
10,001 to 15,000	£1.42 per unit
15,001 to 20,000	£1.16 per unit
20,001 to 50,000	£0.80 per unit
50,001 plus	£0.34 per unit

There's no reason at all why anybody should be unable to store this in their memory bank. It's only *laziness* that stops us.

Look how straightforward the structure is: the price per unit drops by a flat 26p up to the third band of 20,000; the bands themselves are in ranges of five thousand up to this figure. Thereafter the drop in rate is 36p and 46p respectively.

Remember the figure 168; see if you can associate it with something familiar. If you're lucky it may be the house number of somebody close to you, or the first or last three digits of one of your credit cards, for example. The age of your tortoise – anything. It doesn't matter how silly it is. It's for you. It's to help *you* to remember. Equally, the figure 26 may mean something to you: the number of your bus, the year you were born, or someone's birthday. And then it's easy to remember 26 36 46.

To repeat: it's your imagination that always provides the solution. In the above example, it's nothing to do with being good at maths. It's memory. Memory that you've developed through imagination.

7

Tricks with the telephone

As telecommunications become ever more sophisticated in the twenty-first century, that old-timer, the telephone, tends to be taken for granted. The explosion of cellular phones within the population has almost devalued this form of communication. But you must never underestimate it or overlook its value – especially in the professional world. It's usually at the kick-off to your goal. Because it conveys impressions, your 'telephone self' needs to be on top form.

We're all quite different in our manner when telephoning friends, relatives and people we know fairly well. When we use the phone in a business context, we quite naturally observe a different code. Being effective in the workplace often demands good telephone skills. E-mails don't smile or exhibit any 'paralanguage' to enforce impressions.

Used wisely, the phone paves the way for successful meetings and may also avoid the necessity for long trips. For instance, if – clients feel so comfortable and reassured in their dealings with you over the phone that they don't request a face-to-face meeting, you're saving that most precious of commodities: time.

Have you ever come back from a meeting with somebody – a solicitor, planning officer from the local council, a colleague based at another branch, a potential client, an existing client – and said to yourself: 'I could have done all that on the phone'? Three or four hours or even a day or two, with travelling and an overnight stay somewhere could possibly have been avoided by a telephone conversation. This goes on every day, everywhere, because in many cases the person's telephone self is not persuasive enough.

With the rising costs of key personnel, 'downsizing', petrol costs and general time constraints imposed on us all in the present day, the telephone has now become the backbone of many operations. If you can use it to the greatest effect, the dividends are indisputable.

Cultivate a good telephone manner

Problem: some people, including so-called 'professionals', just cannot communicate on the telephone. They seem to undergo a complete change of personality when confronted with a phone call. They become stilted, nervous, incomprehensible, brusque, or even rude, coming across as plain 'hard going'. This is not good when their aim is to sell themselves.

Clients can also have a bad telephone manner. This makes your job that much more difficult.

The problem with any telephone conversation is that you cannot see the person you're speaking to, and therefore cannot observe their body language. Nor can you use facial expressions or body language to enforce your message. That means you must make your voice work much harder than you would have to in a face-to-face situation.

How? By your *choice of words* and *tone of voice*.

People forget that a lot of the words they use when speaking to somebody in person are subconsciously chosen to go with a facial expression or gesture, an accompaniment that gives added meaning to the words.

'You're such a know-all, aren't you?'
'Oh, I don't think I can possibly sign this.'
'How are the results of the advertising campaign?'
'Terrible!'

All of these remarks could be interpreted quite differently over the phone, without the usual accompanying wink or grin to signal humour. Facial expressions can turn an apparent insult into a joke. Over the phone the listener would have to be alert to voice inflections to establish whether a remark was teasing or serious.

It feels unnatural to have to speak without using body language; that's why it's a lesson to watch experienced communicators conversing on the phone. They act naturally. You see them using facial expressions and gesticulating, just as if they were speaking with the other person face-to-face.

This puts *feeling* into the message, which is picked up at the other end of the line. Acting out a conversation gives you the illusion of actually being there. It therefore makes your words more effective. You're not hampered by speaking into a plastic handset, and the changes of facial expression automatically create the right voice pattern. Try it. Experiment: try being angry over the phone with a big smile on your face. Doesn't work, does it?

Exactly the same principles apply to training people to speak on the radio. Professional trainers will invariably tell candidates to make their voices 'smile' whenever appropriate in order to communicate enthusiasm or any other *positive* emotion. This gives colour and character to the unseen speaker's voice and makes its message more likely to be heard. In some organisations you'll see stickers attached to each phone with the message 'Put a smile in your voice'. That's proof enough that people need to pay more attention to their telephone technique.

It's the misguided fear of feeling and looking silly that generally inhibits people smiling into a receiver. So they hide behind a monotone. (Have you ever spoken to a Harley Street consultant – a member of the caring profession – over the phone?) People fail to understand that by using all the other means of expression you enhance your tone of voice and thus your delivery. And telephone is all about *voice*.

Pick the right approach

More often than not we are talking to 'strangers' on the telephone, people whom we've never met. And, more than likely, we're asking them to do things for us. So we have to sell ourselves:

'I know you've got a backlog of jobs, I understand that, but being without electricity, it's so frightening for my four-year-old – she believes in ghosts as well!'

'I really do need to speak to Mr Hyde this morning. Is there a chance you could try and contact him and get him to call me during the coffee break at his conference?'

'I'm more than aware that your time's at a premium this week, Miss Sloane, as you're just back from holiday, but – I think you'll find our meeting very worthwhile if you could find twenty minutes or so on Friday morning.'

What we say and how we deliver are the keys. The way we react to a request depends on the way in which it is made. Consider how the following approaches would affect you:

Telephoning a doctor's receptionist for a home visit:

(a) 'Hello. My son's not feeling too well – his throat's been awful the whole weekend. I'd like the doctor to come round this morning. Or I'll accept between 1.15 and 2 pm. I've got to go to the shops after that. *(More or less a demand).*

(b) 'I know it's Monday morning and the surgery's probably very busy, but I really do need the doctor to come round as soon as possible.' *(A concerned manner, conveying that I can see your point of view too.)*

Chasing up an insurance claim:

(a) 'I want my storm damage claim settled immediately. It's two weeks since I sent it in. I'm not impressed with your company at all.'

(b) 'It's two weeks since I sent my claim form in to you. I know there's been a Bank Holiday and you've probably got trillions of storm damage claims, but this is really causing me problems. Could you settle it quickly?' *(Delivered with feeling.)*

It's obvious which approaches are going to get the best results over the telephone, isn't it? Of course there will always be the exception: where some village is missing an idiot! – and you happen, unfortunately, to locate them at the other end of your phone line.

Practically every day we find ourselves in the situation of having to ask something of somebody: so we have to sell them on the idea of cooperating. In order to achieve the right response you have to sell yourself well.

Business calls

In the business world you may need to telephone to:

1 Find out some information about the company.
2 Find out the name of the person that you need to deal with.
3 Talk to this person.
4 Fix up a meeting (or, in many cases, conclude business).

From start to finish the process has to be handled delicately. First, you're asking someone (a 'stranger') to give you information. Then you're asking to speak to the person who would be dealing with your proposition.

Your first phone encounter is often with the secretary of the decision-maker you want to reach. The secretary, often very powerful as a 'screen', is subconsciously deciding how she feels about you. If your voice is pleasant and smiling, but not sycophantic, it may get you past the first hurdle. (There's

no pretence involved in smiling. If you went to the person's office and saw the secretary, you'd certainly be pleasant and smile. You happen to be present *on the phone*. What's the difference?)

The problem: there are too many people telephoning this busy individual, trying to interest them in propositions. And a lot of these people are bad news. They're just not professional in their approach. Result: 'decision-makers' develop a cocoon around them. You can rarely get through to them directly. They're invariably 'in a meeting', according to their protective secretaries, who request you 'write in or fax'.

The average stress-laden person in business is constantly fighting against time. There aren't enough working hours in the day to deal with internal meetings, dealing with memos, reading e-mails, sorting out personnel problems, reading trade magazines, making out-of-town or overseas visits and meeting visitors. Time is at a premium. So if you manage to get connected to the decision-maker, your story had better be good.

Take the process of making a telephone approach step by step. Your aims are: to gauge whether their organisation may be interested in your proposition; to find out whose 'domain' it falls into, and to be put through to that person if they are there. The stages are:

1 Contact with the switchboard operator (or telephone receptionist).
2 Transfer to the decision-maker's secretary (or someone else in the department).

If the first two steps are effective, continue to:

3 Conversation with the decision-maker.
4 The next appropriate step, e.g., arranging a meeting with him.

This scenario is the pattern most business relationships usually follow at the start. So each step is crucial as a means to the end.

If there is ineffective handling of the situation at any one stage, the whole thing collapses like a house of cards. In general, *you don't get a second chance to make a first impression!*

These principles apply not only in face-to-face situations, but even more so over the telephone. The selling of the 'self' doesn't start at stage 3; it starts right from stage 1. Next we'll look at the stages in detail.

The telephone switchboard

The initial stage can sometimes be a complete nightmare; it can really test your patience. In the present day of voicemails, menu options and other choices it can be a struggle just to get to speak to a human being. Even when you get through this maze you can find yourself getting nowhere fast:

Telephone operator/receptionist: 'Good morning. Oakley Securities. Would you hold please?'

They may come back to you three minutes later with: 'Sorry to keep you. How can I . . . ? Just a moment, I have another call.'

'Great,' you think. 'What's wrong with *my* call?' You never had the chance to utter one word.

Then there's the other type, who allows you the privilege of a few words, then cuts in once they've picked up a key word:

'Good morning. Millennium Sponsorships. How can I help you?'

'Morning. I'd like to know – for your payroll, who would handle . . . *(Click)* the computer software requirements?'

It's too late. The last bit died on your lips. You were transferred when you heard the click.

'Extension 228. Salaries.'

'Oh, good morning. Computer systems for payroll – who handles this?'

'Nothing to do with us, mate. Who put you through?'

'Your switchboard.'

'I'll transfer you back.'

'Yes, but, excuse me can you just . . .' *(Click)*

'Good morning. Millennium Sponsorships. How can . . . ?'

'I spoke to you earlier, I wanted your computer systems people who handle . . .' *(Click)*

'Morning. Systems, John speaking.'

'Oh, hello. I just wanted to speak to the person who deals with the purchase of software for your payroll.'

'That wouldn't be us. You could try Personnel. I can transfer you to switchboard.'

'No, no, that's OK. (*Click* – yours)

Defeat. It happens to us all. As consumers we'll constantly put up with this kind of treatment when trying to obtain 'Customer Service', telephoning to seek out information or trying to make a complaint relating to a product or service. In business life it's par for the course.

Fortunately, not all telephone operators are so hit and miss:

'Good afternoon. CTC. How can I help you?'

'Good afternoon. You could help me by telling me who the travel manager is these days.'

It's difficult to refuse assistance after we've offered it. You subtly remind the switchboard operator of her offer by starting with 'You could help me by . . .'. (Note: 'How can I help you?' is a useful phrase that's gradually crept over from the other side of the Atlantic, and is being used by many organisations now. But if you use it, be prepared to back it up.)

'. . . who the travel manager is these days' implies that you've dealt with the company before. You may have, and even if you haven't it doesn't matter. What matters is the split-second subconscious evaluation in the operator's mind that you've dealt with the company before, and that affords you attention.

'The travel manager is Mr Jenkins,' the operator tells you.

So you've found out who the travel manager is – but you still have to get past his secretary:

'Could I speak to him please?'

'All calls go through to his assistant first.'

'Oh. Could you tell me his or her name please?'

'Yes, it's Sylvia.'

(So irritating! With some calls you'll get a *first* name of an individual, which is not very helpful for you. You can hardly say, when you're put through, 'Oh, hello, Sylvia. Is it possible . . . ?')

'Would you know her second name?'

'Yes. Wright – Sylvia Wright.'

Now you're through to the assistant.

'Mr Jenkins' office. Good afternoon.'

'Would that be Sylvia Wright?'

Yes, speaking.'

The secretary/personal assistant

It's back to the rewards of having the courtesy to remember people's names. You're appealing to the ego. Most secretaries regard themselves as personal assistants to their bosses. Many have just such a title. Switchboard operators and receptionists (especially if they're temps or new to the job) may be unaware of this. Don't do what almost everyone else does and refer to her directly as a secretary. The connotations of this for a real PA with a key role will not endear you to her.

Address her as a person in her own right – with a name – and you will feel an immediate response. You've caught her attention. And psychologically she's predisposed towards you. You've confirmed her identity in the hierarchy, something people strive for in the office jungle every day.

Now for the difficult part. You've confirmed her identity. Next, try to establish *yours*.

It's at this stage that things either progress or fall apart. The trouble is that some individuals who screen calls for a busy boss take things too far. Their over-protectiveness can mean that their bosses don't get to hear about something that could be of interest. You have to increase your efforts to ensure that you get a hearing.

There are certain prerequisites, such as courtesy. There's no substitute. We like talking to personable, well-mannered people; there's a shortage, so if you exhibit courtesy you're halfway there. Most people are too lazy and can't be bothered. The next issue is, do you sound important? (All right, you *are* important, but that's not the point.) Do you sound important? That's all the screener has got to go by. She can't assess your outward appearance on the telephone: you're judged on how you sound, what you say and how you say it.

Let's continue. You've just asked if Mr Jenkins is free:

'Could you tell me what it's in connection with?'

'Yes, of course. It's MBI International . . . My name's Harrison, I have to discuss a conference package with him.'

'Has he spoken to you before, Mr Harrison?'

'No, we haven't spoken yet.'

'I'll see if he's free.'

After two minutes: 'He's rather tied up at the moment. Could you write in, perhaps?'

'It's not that simple. I need to actually discuss something with him, Miss Wright; I don't mind holding on. I only need four or five minutes of his time.'

'Just a moment, Mr Harrison.'

'Jenkins speaking.'

She's let you through the filter. Well done. But don't forget that bosses themselves can also relish playing hard to get! They feel powerful when they refuse to take calls. It gives them a sense of satisfaction. ('People want to talk to me, but I just haven't got the time' – *self-esteem boost*).

They also think it necessary to keep impressing upon their secretaries that they're not prepared to talk to all and sundry. However, there's no denying the fact that assistants wield great influence. You have to sell yourself to them.

Look at it from their point of view. They don't want to look inefficient to their boss; they have to be selective about who is allowed access. In reality, some carry this too far, so it's up to the caller to create the right impression and then to persist – pleasantly.

A boss may ask his secretary for a thumbnail evaluation (thirty seconds) of the intruder on the phone and what the call is about. Then it's up to her to sell him the idea of talking to you ('He seems very nice Mr Jenkins. It might be worth having a quick word with him'). And suddenly she's involved in your goal of selling yourself!

Chatting up the decision-maker

When you eventually get through to the person you're aiming for, you are effectively a *guest* on his telephone line; you should conduct your conversation with that in mind.

You've certainly interrupted this individual in the middle of something. You don't know what kind of mood he's in. He could be at the height of a crisis. He may have just come back from an overseas trip that morning. He could be recovering from an illness. His roof at home might have blown off in a gale. He might be in the middle of a meeting. But whatever it is, you can be sure he won't tell you. It's up to you now. Use some of that ESP. Where's your empathy – the quality most people are short of? Get inside the mind.

'Mr Jenkins – thank you for your time. I'll be brief.'

Two Brownie points. You've acknowledged that he's busy. That's courteous. Second, you've made a positive move towards ensuring that you get his attention while you're talking. You've promised to be *brief*. Music to his ears!

You know how it is. Somebody that you already know comes on the line. You've got a million things to do. If you know that person is inclined to go on and on, your mind says: 'Oh no, not him again.' Consequently you switch off, and all the time the caller is speaking you're distracted because you're trying to work out which sentence will be the last. *So you miss most of what's being said.*

So often, people take a phone call from a caller under sufferance, either because they find it difficult to say no, or because they've refused many times before and they feel they ought to put the person off for good. A negative situation from the outset, it starts to resemble a fencing match.

But when the caller says 'I'll be brief', the other person is more likely to drop his guard. They can afford to pay attention and listen. They relax a little and actually hear what's being said.

Certain types of people prefer you to get to the point quickly. Their own minds race away with what's being discussed, and it's no good you being left on the starting block. (This type will feature in a later chapter when we discuss personality types.)

Many people prolong a telephone call by speaking in a slow monotone, throwing out sentences and failing to finish them because they've thought of something else. Their conversations, or monologues, go something like this: 'Maybe we can try and . . . I mean if you're able to contract to a minimum of . . . Or I suppose I could see what I could do . . .' And it goes on and on. There's no beginning, no end – no result.

You may get away with this in a face-to-face situation where you may be seen to have compensatory qualities. But of course, on the phone you rely solely on the projection of your message.

Ask yourself, 'What's happening on the other end of the line?'

At the other end of the line

It happens to everybody, all the time. You may be at home, in absolute agony: 'Come on Scully . . . if you don't crack the code of the ancient artifact, Mulder will die of the deadly virus. No, don't go in there . . . aliens . . . No, don't!'

The telephone rings. You grab the remote and turn down the volume on the TV set. Cursing the interruption, you force yourself to the phone and snap out a 'Hello':

'Oh, is that you, John? It's Tom here.'

'Tom – hi.'

'You sounded different. Anyway, listen. I had to ring you. Remember we were talking about that hotel in Venice last month? . . . Oh, just a minute, John. Get away, Samantha, Daddy's on the phone. Go and help Mummy move your toys. No, you can't . . . Sorry, John – interruptions all the time. Now, where was I? How's things with you both, anyway? Ok?'

'Yeah, yeah. Er . . . not bad.' *(Mega brusque)*

'Can you remember the name of that hotel, then, John?'

'What hotel?' *(Glancing at the silent TV set)*

'The hotel in Venice. The one facing the canal.'

The conversation continues in the same vein.

This kind of sitation occurs every day, at home and in the office. Can you imagine Tom, after the call, when his wife asks him, 'Well, how was John? Did he remember the name of the hotel?'

'Mmm – he was a bit strange.'

'Oh. What d'you mean by "strange"?'

'Well, he was a bit brusque, not his usual pleasant self.'

'You don't think Joanna's left him?'

'No, no.'

'Maybe we've upset him. You don't owe him any money, do you? Or have we borrowed something that we haven't returned? Maybe he didn't like his birthday present – I thought it was quite appropriate.'

'No, no. I don't think it's anything like that. Anyway, he definitely was a bit odd. He didn't seem to be paying attention to what I was saying. Just wasn't interested.'

'Well, maybe they had company. Did you ask him?'

'No, I didn't. Hey – you know, you could be right. Just before he hung up he was mumbling something about a "Dana Scully"!'

What a situation. Both parties are left feeling disturbed by the call. Tom is cursing John for making him miss the important bit of *The X Files*, and Tom is inwardly annoyed with John. ('Well, if he can't be half decent when I call him for a friendly chat, even if he did have company, he can forget it.) Later on, after the TV programme is over, John may analyse the telephone conversation (what conversation?) and think to himself: 'Mmm, maybe I was a bit – short with Tom. No – he wouldn't have taken offence.'

The problem is very simple: when you telephone somebody, at work or home, you are bound to be interrupting them as they are gardening, writing a report, surfing the Internet, eating a meal, having an argument or a meeting, in a crisis situation, watching television . . . But some interruptions are much worse than others.

Just imagine if Tom had used his head to get inside your mind once he'd picked up on your rather curt greeting:

'John, it's Tom here. Am I interrupting something? Can you talk?'

'Well, it's OK. I'm just watching *The X Files*; it's the last episode of this series.'

'Hey, listen, I'll call you back at nine. It's not life or death. I'll talk to you later.'

'But . . .'

'No, don't worry. Talk to you at nine. Bye for now.'

What a different scenario to the previous one. You are impressed by Tom showing such empathy. It doesn't fail to register. And you'll almost certainly be the one to make the call at 9 pm, before Tom does. And he'll be all ears, too!

People don't concentrate on what you're saying if their minds are elsewhere. You're being two-timed again. It can't be repeated often enough. The effectiveness of your message over the phone will be at its optimum only if the other party is paying *full attention*.

Most people don't let on that you're interrupting them or that you've caught them at a bad time. It's up to you to detect it from their tone of voice – remember telephone is all about voice – then decide what to do. *You* must take the lead; it's in *your* interest.

Timing

If you catch a person at the wrong time, it could be the end of your relationship, your sale, your pay rise, your request for an urgent call-out to the plumber, your trip to a trade fair, your request to have a day off. And you usually don't get a second chance. Remember the point made earlier: people don't generally like to change their minds after refusing a request. It makes them look indecisive and appear as though they made a mistake in the first instance (ego again). Even if they know that they were wrong, they may stick rigidly to their original decision, which may have been made hastily.

Why was it made in haste? Because they were *busy* and wanted to get rid of you. If you had picked up the vibes and offered to call back . . . *different story perhaps*. Let's face it. Sometimes it's easier in life to say no immediately, if you're pushed for time and preoccupied.

So timing is all-important. If you can tell from a person's strained voice that it's not a convenient time, and therefore unconducive to your cause, nip the conversation in the bud. Sometimes the other party does it, but in most instances it will have to be you. You may have more to lose.

This point is so important (and so neglected) that it deserves repetition: knowing *when* and *when not* to speak to somebody on the telephone can make the difference between moving mountains and molehills.

When the other person has company

Quite often when you call someone in an office, they are with another person. They may tell you this, and suggest that either one of you rings back later:

'I'm in the middle of a meeting at the moment. Can I call you back?'

'I have someone with me. Can you call back later?'

If, as in the first example, they offer to ring you back, say that *you* will call. It's better that way. They are quite likely to forget. You will save yourself waiting and wondering. Even if they haven't forgotten, your call may now be low priority (with all the problems that have emerged from the meeting you interrupted). It's at basement level in their in-tray.

If the other person tells you that they are with someone, you're lucky. More often than not, you won't be told. That's where the trouble starts.

Problem: *people talk differently on the phone when someone is with them*. The reasons include:

1 They are nervous.
2 They want to impress the person who is with them.
3 They're conscious that they're keeping the person with them waiting (and therefore hurry the conversation).
4 They don't want the person present to know about the topic being discussed.
5 They're speaking through an intercom phone (and their audience can hear your every word).

Catch yourself when you are alone, talking in the privacy of your own home or office. Your telephone conversation is probably quite fluent, as you gaze at your familiar surroundings. You don't have to watch what you say at your end. Nobody can hear you. It's a private conversation between two people.

Now compare this situation to one in which you are with another person, or a group of people. You may adopt a more officious tone; you may be less friendly; less 'playful', even. Your words are chosen more carefully, so you become less *natural* and less *fluent*. You're conscious that your dialogue is being 'vetted' by the other person present. It's natural.

If you are phoning somebody for the first time, to try to gain their interest, and they happen to have somebody with them, you could have problems. They may be the type that's always ready to impress the person present. It could be their boss that is in with them. So they may try to 'kick you around'. It's done for show. Their audience see a bravado display that says: 'I know how to handle potential time-wasters. My time is important.'

You may be a nice person. Your telephone manner may be excellent, your proposition wonderful. But there'll be an artificial rejection of your call because the other person wants to look clever and powerful in front of their onlookers.

If they're having a meeting of some sort, a phone call forces a break in the proceedings. Meetings have various levels of importance. Their secretary, partners, chairman, advertising agency, or liquidator could be in the office. It would be fine if they told you to call back. But many people *don't*, often because they think it will be an inconvenience to them (or to you).

If they do take your call, their concentration is wavering because they're aware of keeping the people in their office waiting. Their time is valuable too. The easiest way to get you off the line is to say no to your proposal, regardless of its merit.

Sometimes, your call may be a confidential follow-up to something you've already discussed. They don't want the person present to know that they're thinking of buying a cottage in the Dordogne, or an office jacuzzi, or considering hiring consultants for a project. Their conversation with you thus becomes stilted and monosyllabic, and you think they're no longer interested.

It's important to bear in mind that if a person you're calling has company, you have to work hard to read their tone of voice. This will give you a pointer as to whether you should risk a quick shot at your request or proposition, or wait for a more favourable opportunity.

If you're speaking to somebody for the first time, it's as well to ask if it's convenient to talk. Even if you've passed through the 'filter' and they have agreed to speak, this gesture can make the person more responsive.

The golden rule is: *assess whether the time is right to make your request or put forward your proposition, or whether you would get a better hearing at some other time.*

How many times have you come off the phone and thought to yourself: 'That's strange. He was interested when we met last week; what could have happened? He sounded completely diferent, tense, almost.' (And how many times have people thought that about you?)

He probably sounded different and less receptive because he wasn't alone. You should assess the situation and cut it short. If you go ahead regardless and risk having your say, perhaps when telephoning someone for the first time, if it's the wrong moment, you may lose out and never have another opportunity.

The moral: if you're in any doubt, ask if you're interrupting something. You're getting inside the mind. You're showing your powers of ESP (empathy, sincerity, perspicacity).

Timing is vital in the persuasion game. We will often respond to the same approach completely differently at different times; it's human nature. Sometimes the reason is cognitive (mood), sometimes it's circumstance. It should be stressed again and again: bringing something up at the wrong time can lay it to rest forever. Waiting until the right opportunity can lead you straight to your goal.

You know all about timing in your home life. You'll wait until the time is right before you bring up anything important:

'Darling, sit down. Shall I get you a glass of Chardonnay? There you are. How was the meeting today? It went well! I'm so glad. The prospect of a salary increase from next month? That's wonderful news . . . Another glass? There you are. You know you said you were going to take time off in September? Well, Emily showed me this Mediterranean cruise offer that was in the *Daily Mail*.'

In the working world, much potential business is lost because the caller cannot understand the need to be intuitive before pitching on the phone. Would you ring a potential client at 9.15 on their first morning back from a two-week summer holiday (about something you discussed almost on the eve of their departure)? Would you call your boss, the managing director, about your adventurous choice of a new company car, on the morning they discover that the company is the subject of an unwelcome takeover bid?

People generally respond better if they're in a good mood and not under pressure, and when things are going fairly well. Show some perspicacity. Time your requests to your advantage. In other words, call when the other person is able to give their best attention. Good thinking is essential in personal relationships, and it's crucial in the business world. We should constantly be aware of this. We know it's true.

Introducing yourself on the phone

You've got through to Mr Jenkins. So take things one step at a time. You know that using his name will make the whole approach more personal. You want him to remember your name, and your company's name – or, at worst, one of the two. Research has shown that most people contacted by phone are more concerned about missing the company name than that of the caller. They don't mind asking for your name at the end of the call (if they've got empathy, and can be bothered, they'll want to know your name at the outset so they can be courteous and address you by it).

The problem: on getting through to Mr Right, most people blurt out both names in one elongated phrase (often mumbled): 'Hello, it's James Harrison of MBI International here. I wondered if we might meet to discuss . . . (no pause for breath). Sometimes almost as if they are ashamed, people feel obliged to speak as fast as possible – to get the petty details out of the way. Petty? Your name, the company's name? Hardly.

Get this straight. We live in a world in which we spend most of our income on 'wants' rather than just 'needs'. We usually have to be informed about those products and services that we later designate as 'wants' – a superior over-head projector, infra-red night torch, new breakfast cereal, sponsorship of a sporting event, etc.

When you're calling a potential client you may have a product or service to sell that could be a real asset to them – and their organisation (in that order). There's no room for lack of self-esteem. A potential client would often prefer that you justified their time (and your own) spent speaking on the phone and fix up a meeting. After all, nobody likes to miss out. You might have some interesting ideas.

So when you introduce yourself by phone to a stranger, be aware of how much their mind can take in at once. You want your identity firmly established. So say it *slowly*: 'Mr Jenkins. Good morning.' Pause. 'It's MBI International here.' Pause again. Let him assimilate and remember. Let his mental computer do a rapid search for recognition. Now that the first bit has sunk in, you can state your name: 'My name's James Harrison.'

Think about it. You give the person a chance to either

recall or register the name of your company. Then you give them the opportunity to hear your name and therefore *remember* it. Result: they don't feel as if they're talking to just a *voice*. That's better for you because:

It's *easy* to reject a *voice*.
It's *harder* to reject a *person*.

Just think of a call you've had from somebody who rattled off their name and organisation. If you're preoccupied you may have missed both pieces of information. You don't feel any rapport with the person speaking and, as you're busy anyway, the inclination is: 'How do I get this voice off my line?'

To recap: you've said you'll be brief; Mr Jenkins has computed that. You've given the name of your organisation; he's computed that. And then your name; hopefully he'll remember it, but, if not, it's easy for him to say, later on in the conversation: 'I'm sorry, I didn't catch the name.'

There's every chance too that if you enunciate clearly and pace your words, the listener will feel like writing down these 'important' details while you're passing them on.

Setting up a meeting

Right. You've sorted out the identity problem. Now you want to see if you can arouse interest in your services and perhaps arrange a meeting. But remember that before people will agree to see you, they want to be reasonably sure about some key points:

1 That they like the sound of you – and therefore of what you stand for.
2 That your product or service shows promise. So they're not wasting time that could be better spent on a pressing report, important meeting, on the golf course, or whatever. There is sacrifice involved, after all.
3 That you would be easy to get rid of, if there is no common ground. This is a very important consideration, and cannot be stressed too much. Many meetings never happen because

of a pushy attitude over the phone. The person thinks: 'If I can't get this person off the phone, what would he be like once he'd infiltrated my office (or home)?' So, although they may well be interested, they are put off the whole idea.

Nobody really likes saying no – especially in person. It's easier on the telephone; one can fence and say, 'Send me some literature' and end the matter there. When telephoned again, the secretary can say that her boss has looked at it and he isn't interested 'at the moment' but 'We'll put it on file and . . .'. The equivalent of Hollywood's 'Don't call us – we'll call you.'

Because the other person needs to feel comfortable about being able to say no after a face-to-face meeting, how you come across on the phone determines whether or not they agree to meet you. If you show that you're willing to invest time you've got a good chance.

Yet so many people fail to get that all-important first meeting because they cannot see the psychological reasoning behind this. They mistake aggression for confidence. There's nothing wrong with being confident about your services; in fact, it's a prerequisite. But there's a thin line between just enough confidence and too much.

They also mistake enthusiasm for confidence. Again, there's nothing wrong with being enthusiastic, but some people go over the top. It gives the whole conversation an air of falsity. It puts the other person off. They end up refusing to see you. They're thinking: 'I wouldn't mind knowing about this service – could be useful, especially as we're reviewing the people we use at the moment, since they let us down recently. But this guy's irritating. I'll never get rid of him if I see him; he'll hound me.' It's the caller's attitude that's to blame. They didn't sell themselves well. Did he get inside the mind? No. The person refused to meet him for a negative reason. And that's tragic.

Short is good

Being told at the beginning of the telephone call that it would be brief, that made Mr Jenkins relax. How about using the same tactic when trying to arrange your meeting?

'I understand, Mr Jenkins, that you're involved in the arrangements for your company's fiftieth anniversary celebrations.'

'Yes, I am.'

'I've a feeling we met at a seminar about a year or so ago, if my memory for names is accurate.'

'MBI, did you say?'

'Yes.'

'Wasn't it at the conference in the Empress Suite at Brighton? In the Grand hotel, that super five-star along the seafront? I think it was during afternoon tea in the lounge that I bumped into you.'

'Yes, it was. I was convinced your name sounded familiar. Small world! I'm calling because I'd like to fix up a short meeting, half an hour or so. Ideally, within the next two weeks.'

'Well, this week's bad. Next week . . . Let me see – any time except Tuesday afternoon and Thursday morning.'

'OK. How about Monday, three o'clock?'

'That's fine. I'm writing it in my diary now. MBI . . . Mister . . . ?'

'Harrison – James Harrison.'

'Right, Mr Harrison. See you then. Nice to have spoken to you. Thank you for calling.'

'Thank you. I'll just drop you a note confirming. Look forward to the ninth at three o'clock. Bye.'

Very amicable. If only more calls were like that. But the point is this: we can usually steer any call in the right direction by figuring out how people's minds work.

Analyse: 'a short meeting, half an hour or so'. As well as being music to Jenkins' ears, this delivers a double message:

1 You are implying: 'My time is valuable too, because I'm *successful*. And I'm successful because I'm *good*.'
2 Your exit will be painless (for him). He won't have to use body language hints to get rid of you.

These two factors are bound to encourage a successful meeting.

Analyse: 'Ideally, within the next two weeks'. Notice the flexibility of the meeting date. You are giving Mr Jenkins most of the control. 'Ideally' suggests 'no pressure', but it's a subtle indication of your preference.

If you follow a similar procedure to the one outlined above, you will certainly have done everything possible to clinch that important first meeting. (When the time comes, the meeting may well go on for longer than half an hour – but not at your instigation, at the other person's. Because they are so relaxed they end up asking all sorts of supplementary questions. And after they've agreed a contract with you, they may apologise to you on the way out – for taking up too much of *your* time!)

8

Making words work for you: the power of psycholinguistics

Do you overlook the *power* of words in your dealings in everyday life? Are you aware how some words seem to 'work' and others don't? Do you choose your words carefully and monitor their effect? Not enough attention is paid to the subtleties of making effective word associations, considering the different outcomes that are possible when words and phrases are constructed and delivered in alternative ways.

Researchers in *psycholinguistics*, a branch of psychology devoted to the study of verbal behaviour, observe how we use language and how verbal abilities interact with other cognitive abilities – how words affect our minds and emotions.

Language can influence thought, and words are the tools we can use to create mental images. We're always reminded of how politicians use 'double-speak' – language that is deliberately used to confuse, mislead, conceal and distort meaning. An economic slump may be described as 'negative economic growth', and a PVC wallet as 'imitation leather'! Words can be used to shape and, sometimes distort, the way that we think.

Think about it. You want to convey something to somebody. You have in your mind an image which you translate into words. The other person takes your words and translates them back into an image – their *own* image. They decide what it means. The interpretation takes place inside their mind.

If the other person's mental picture doesn't correspond to yours, communication has not been effective. The word associations sparked off by your choice of words may produce a negative result.

How a person feels is determined by their interpretations. As human beings we (in the following order):

1 *sense*,
2 *interpret*,
3 *feel*.

So we are able to control what we feel by the simple act of changing our *interpretations* (the basis of much cognitive therapy); this changes our feelings. Not an easy task, but it can be done. So much of what we hear or read can be misinterpreted through bad choice of words. 'That's not what I mean(t)' is something that you're probably used to hearing in arguments at home and in other areas of your life.

That is why it is so important to get *feedback* from the listener. Making verbal communication effective and clear involves both the sender of the message and the receiver.

Choose your words with care

Consider the following example, in which Amanda leaves a message on her friend Sally's answerphone – which should she use?

(a) 'I won't be able to come to the Royal Festival Hall on Saturday, Sally. You'll have to try and sell my ticket. I'll pay you if you can't. John's back and he's taking me out. Sorry about that. Talk to you soon. Bye.' *(Sally had queued to get the tickets weeks ago.)*

(b) 'Sally, isn't it great? John's been given a weekend off from his job in New York. He wants to take me out. Doesn't know when he'll get over again. So I can't make the concert on Saturday. I can understand if you're disappointed – I'm sorry, I was really looking forward to it. Perhaps you can try and sell the ticket. Otherwise don't worry, I'll pay you back. I hope we can arrange something else soon. Bye for now.'

Which one will be less of a blow to her friend? The message and request are essentially the same. But (a) would leave

Sally feeling a little rejected. Too much of 'me' and not enough concern for her. The second message starts off in an enthusiastic, positive way. Then it goes on to explain further and acknowledge Sally's possible feelings. A little thought on Amanda's part and the relationship will remain on a better footing. The first message has forty-three words and the second seventy-nine. Hardly a great sacrifice in terms of time.

Of course, human nature being so complex, it's impossible to know exactly how particular words will be interpreted and thus received. But if we can get inside the mind of the individual, we can choose the words that will have the best chance of achieving the desired effect.

Another example: A personnel manager is standing in the corridor with the managing director. He says to a passing secretary: 'Have you seen Tom Collins? We need to discuss the training budget'.

'Yes,' she replies. 'As a matter of fact I saw him about ten minutes ago, tottering up the stairs towards Accounts.'

It's now two-thirty, so the personnel manager assumes Collins has been for a 'liquid lunch'. His mind has latched on to the word 'tottering', with all its implications. He has a mental image of Collins being below par, and doesn't want to risk the MD seeing Collins in this state, so he makes an excuse for deferring the meeting.

In fact, there are a number of possible explanations:

1 The secretary used the word 'tottering' simply because it was the first one to come into her head. She had actually meant to say 'trotting', but it came out as 'tottering'. (Perhaps *she* had the liquid lunch!)
2 Collins had been weight-training or playing squash during his lunch break, so he looked and felt tired.
3 He was suffering from a bad attack of migraine.

However, the use of that one 'throwaway' word introduced a *negative* association. The personnel manager now sees Collins as someone who drinks too much at lunchtime. It is a mistaken impression, formed by a single word, but the idea has taken root. An assumption incorrectly brands somebody as a drunkard.

Let's take a further example. A solicitor is annoyed at the unusually poor quality of his secretary's typing. The number of serious mistakes is becoming intolerable.

He tells her: 'Sandra, your typing's very shoddy lately. It's important that the invoices are accurate when they go out. It's very difficult to get clients to pay up on any shortfall if it's due to our mistakes.'

The instant Sandra hears the word 'shoddy', her blood pressure rises and she becomes defensive. She's bitter at the personal affront.

'Doesn't he know,' she seethes, 'that those two extra staff transferred from the City are giving me lots of contracts to type? I'm snowed under! How am I supposed to cope? Doesn't he consider that? I only stay here out of a misguided sense of loyalty. He can keep his invoices. He can keep his job!' *(Exit stage left.)*

The solicitor would probably still have Sandra on his payroll if his approach had been something like this:

'Sandra, your typing's not up to its usual impressive standard. Any problems?'

This is an invitation for the secretary to offer reasons, and she naturally wants to justify not reaching her normal 'impressive standard':

'Well, Mr Keen, I'm sorry if you think that. The truth is, I just can't cope. I don't know whether it's been brought to your attention, but the two gentlemen from the City office have been giving me at least six detailed contracts to type every day.'

'Oh, I didn't realise. If invoices go out with errors it holds up payment. Also it's difficult to get the clients to pay up if there's a shortfall due to our error. OK, I'll see if their typing can be done by Mrs . . .'

Net result: he's had a chance to compliment and criticise (nicely) and Sandra will strive to reach her former 'impressive standard'. (Oh, and the solicitor still has a secretary!)

'It ain't what you say . . .'

Studying how words affect our minds and emotions is fascinating, because we are constantly in communication with people, reading, writing, listening and speaking. Surely a moment's thought as to how a word or phrase may be interpreted by another person is worth the effort? The wrong choice of word has precipitated many wars, divorces, fights, arguments and business bust-ups.

Remember we are all practitioners of persuasion, and our basic tools are words. But, like all good craftsmen, we have to know which are the right ones to select from the toolkit for the job in hand. It's usually laziness that prevents people from doing this. It's easier to just leave the brain in low gear and say:

> 'I disagree totally with what you're saying.'
> 'I'm not happy with your work.'
> 'I'm afraid we can't deliver for eight weeks.'
> 'I regret to inform you . . .'
> 'You must tell me how much you're paying at the moment if we're to . . .'
> 'Bad news. I've spoken to the engineer and the earliest he can come out is . . .'

People spend their time 'brainwashing' others that things are worse than they really are. Why do they do it? They make it hard for themselves by creating bad feeling, when there needn't be any. Get inside the mind.

There are much *better* ways of phrasing the preceding statements. How about:

> 'Won't you look at this way and imagine it from my point of view?'
> 'Any reason why we're getting more complaints for your section?'
> 'We'll get your jogging machine to you sometime within the next eight weeks'.
> 'We have to tell you . . .'

'It would be helpful if I knew how much . . .'

'The engineer's busy but he knows it's important to you and he'll get out to you by . . .'

If you've ever played the word-association game, you'll know how your mind triggers off an image in the subconscious. It's quite automatic. A word evokes a certain feeling and a picture in the mind.

So make sure the message you're communicating is conveyed in the right words and also at the right time. Certain words may be appropriate at one time but not another. You are then far more likely to get the result you are after.

We're not talking about deception, but about *perception*. Using the right tools for the right job, understanding the psycholinguistic connotations of saying things in certain ways.

Questions, questions

The way we phrase questions to draw out information from other people is crucial. Questioning is an important skill that is needed in communicating successfully. There are *open* questions and there are *closed* questions.

The open question uses words in such a way that the respondent answers in more detail and at greater length. For example, if I said to you: 'Do you like horror films?' (closed question), your answer may be short and specific. 'What sort of films do you like?' (open question) would probably elicit a fuller, longer reply.

Open questions are useful for 'getting inside the mind', as they encourage self-disclosure. You can use them to find out a person's true, possibly hidden, motives or desires.

Those good old indispensables *What? When? How? Where?* and *Who?* are also good problem-solving tools. They too encourage people to reveal their innermost feelings. (There may be a general reluctance to use these old favourites, for fear of appearing too forward. Correct delivery helps overcome this problem.)

Like open questions, these are effective questions for getting inside the mind. But the way in which they are asked, and the rapport (or lack of it) that has already been established will determine their effect. They will obviously be more successful if you have managed to strike up some empathy with the person you are dealing with.

People often ask why we exclude *Why?* from the list. The reason is that it requires a rational explanation for our behaviour. We often don't know why we do or did things. If asked, our inclination is to be defensive. 'Why?' makes us want to *justify* ourselves, rather than look at possible alternatives for the future.

Also, the word is synonymous with criticism:

'Why did you take that road? It would have been much quicker to . . .'

'Why can't you be more careful when you . . . ?'

'Why is your desk always the untidiest in the whole department?'

Criticism and advice deter people from analysing the reasons for their behaviour.

Don't be negative

Research shows that the word '*you*' can be responsible for much negative communication. Used in an accusing way, it can completely alter the course of a conversation and evoke a hostile reaction in the recipient:

'You always have to have the last word, don't you?'

'You never ring when you say you're going to.'

'You ought to go out and find yourself a job.'

'You always let me down when there's an important meeting coming up.'

Far better to rephrase statements like these and alter the feelings that the other person experiences. Replace a defensive response with one that is more constructive than destructive.

Using a more open style of communication should encourage discussion, too.

What about:

'It seems as though the last word generally comes from your direction.'

'I always seem to expect a call from you on a certain day and it never comes.'

'I think it might be a good time now to look for that job.'

' I need your cooperation when I've got important meetings.'

Notice how much less antagonistic this sounds and how the emphasis has shifted to 'I', making you more assertive. You're now much more likely to be listened to by the other person.

A true story

An advertising executive, Mr X, wanted to attend a six day conference in Las Vegas. The conference fee and travel expenses would add up to quite an expensive trip. His boss, Mr Y, was the type who didn't like spending the company's money. (He had a sign above his desk that read: 'I have enough money to last me the rest of my life, unless I want to buy something!)

If he authorised any expense, Mr Y would always want to see an immediate return. Furthermore, if people went on overseas trips, it had to be work, work, work all the way.

Mr X knew that the month of July (when the conference was being held) was a fairly slack time for the company and for himself. So the timing was good, in his eyes. He felt that he might overcome the cost objection by telling his boss that many of his counterparts in other advertising agencies would be there.

But he feared that one factor would kill his plan stone dead: *Las Vegas*. It was bound to conjure up a totally unsuitable image in the mind of his boss: gambling, scantily clad showgirls, Caesar's Palace – anything but a serious conference. Las Vegas just happened to be the venue (although obviously it was part of the attraction of going). So Mr X decided that when he went to sell the idea of the conference to his boss, he would choose his words carefully and focus attention on the convenient date in the calendar and would mention the country (USA) rather than the specific venue.

This is how the meeting went:

'Come in. Sit down.'

'Thanks. I'll get to the point quickly. I was wondering – July is quite slack here for us, and the ADM conference takes place then, in America. I'd like to go. It would be useful for us to have representation there. A lot of blue-chip client companies might be there – good for contacts. A lot of agencies are sending at least one person.'

'Mmm . . . How much?'

'Well, delegate fee plus travel . . . Suppose three to three and a half thousand.'

'That's quite expensive. You say a lot of other agencies are sending somebody? Mmm . . . You know we're over on the T&E budget already?'

'Yes, I know. But I really feel this would be a good year to attend. There's a two-day seminar on . . .'

'Hey, I've got an idea. If you could use the parent company's apartment on Manhattan East Side . . . Yeah, that would cut down on accommodation costs.'

'Oh – but that's in New York.'

'Well, that's where the conference is, isn't it? That's what you said.'

'No, I didn't.'

(Interesting how association is already at work in Mr Y's mind. Mr X only mentioned 'America' but his boss's mind was racing away for a solution. He assumed the venue was New York and even accused Mr X of having said so!)

'Well, where *is* it being held?'

Mr X thought he was cornered; it looked as though his cause was lost. Then he had a brainwave (psycholinguistic solution).

'Where is it? Oh – Nevada.'

'Nevada. Oh . . . yes, Nevada.' (*Pause*). 'That's West Coast, isn't it? Er . . . do they have an airport there?'

'Oh yes. And domestic flights are cheap, too.'

'Well . . . Look, I've got a meeting in five minutes. That's OK then, but keep the costs down, will you?'

'Thanks. I will.'

A happy ending.

Look at what happened, and the thinking behind the moves:

1 Mr X anticipated the association that Las Vegas would conjure up in his boss's mind.

2 So he decided to just mention 'America'.

3 He came unstuck because his boss *imagined* he'd said 'New York'. (Many people have poor memories – remember?)

4 He had to say where the venue was now. So he said 'Nevada'. It was the truth. The conference *was* in Nevada.

This was perfectly all right. It was up to his boss if he wanted to know more. The point is, Mr X probably would not have been booking a plane ticket if he had mentioned Las Vegas.

He had to get inside the mind of his boss and anticipate his interpretation of the idea. Having got over this hurdle, he then emphasised that domestic flights were cheap. This was not too relevant, in the scheme of things, but it struck the final chord as far as his boss was concerned.

So, back to basics. Psychology has given us the label of 'psycholinguistics', but what we're talking about are things we should be aware of every day: how words affect our responses; and the selective, tactful use of words *to get the desired results*.

You could say that, in the above example, Mr X helped his boss to make a particular decision. As already stated: we often want to be persuaded to take a particular course of action. We're looking for a good reason to do it and we just want someone to convince us. Their skilful use of words may tip the balance.

You have to use words to communicate. You may as well choose the best.

9

Personality 'types'

Psychological research into the subject of personality has centred on the aspect of personality traits. Psychological *typing* categorises a number of *related* personality traits. There is almost universal agreement that we are a product of both nature (biology) and nurture (experience).

It was the psychologist Carl Jung who maintained (in contrast to his colleague Freud) that humans are not merely shaped by past events but also progress beyond their past. He maintained that part of the nature of humans is to be constantly developing, growing, and moving toward a balanced and complete level of development. Our present personality, he claimed, is determined both by who and what we have been and also by the person we hope to become.

A keen observer of human behaviour, Jung noticed the diversity between personalities and also the consistency *within* a given personality. He could see by the way different people approached new situations that there were definite 'types' within the population. Some people are cautious and circumspect, while others are daring and adventurous. His major contribution was the concept of *introversion–extraversion*, which is worth exploring, as its meaning is commonly misunderstood.

Jung maintained that every personality directs its psychic energy towards what he called 'introversion–extraversion'. An attitude of introversion turns a person toward their inner or subjective world, where the source of energy is within and comes from solitary experiences. They don't necessarily need external sources for fulfilment. Interaction with people can often be debilitating at times. The attitude of extraversion, by contrast, is an outgoing one in which the *external* world is all-important, and people and material things are significant. According to Jung, even though these attitudes are opposite, each person possesses *both*, and one attitude is dominant over the other. The dominant one is expressed in conscious behaviour while the subordinate one is representative of the person's unconscious.

As we go about our everyday lives, we meet people who are open and friendly; the label 'extraversion' would probably apply to them. This does not mean that they are any more emotional or caring than those with an introversion perspective, who may be more reserved in a social setting. They may be quite adept at dealing with people, but less relaxed with strangers; they may need to know people well and may prefer smaller numbers. You've probably come across people socially or in the workplace who aren't that comfortable in the wine bar or pub at lunchtime with a large group, but are completely different one-to-one or in a very small group.

Extraverts tend to respond quickly to situations and often speak without thinking properly. In meetings at work, or perhaps at seminars, this type of person will make themselves noticed, whereas introverts are usually more cautious by nature and think more about what they are going to say. It doesn't mean they talk any less, as observing those with an introversion preference in a one-to-one situation will show.

There are advantages in being an 'E' (extravert) or an 'I' (introvert). The E person may get more out of life in terms of happiness and satisfaction due to greater *interaction* with other people and a better support system. The I person is less reliant on other people for self-fulfilment, and their image is often one of being attentive and sincere (even if that's not the case!). As far as disadvantages go, the E can be a bit over-bearing sometimes and come across as superficial, while the I may be criticised for poor conversation skills and an apparent lack of interest in certain situations. Jung's observation was that we all use both types. For example, a person is quite capable of being outgoing at work, and more self-absorbed away from that setting.

The other important contribution by Jung was his analysis of the four functions that relate to how we come to know the world and understand it:

1 Thinking
2 Feeling
3 Sensing
4 Intuiting

Although we have the capacity to engage in all of these functions or *traits*, as with introversion–extraversion, we tend to rely on one or two of them. They help to define our personality.

Decision-making and personality types

More recent research into personality types can add to the findings of Jung and help us to identify ourselves and those we are dealing with. You will meet people all the time who have to make decisions after hearing *your* point of view. It can be useful to bear in mind what type of person they are:

1 The person who engages in thinking (*T*) relies on intellectual processes and ideas. A decision is based on the *logical* results of actions and they will decide impersonally.
2 The person who engages in feeling (*F*) uses an evaluative process whereby things are judged pleasing or painful. Decisions will be based on their personal values, on what matters or is important to them or to other people. The keyword is '*emotion*' for this type of person; logic may not play a significant part.

For the T, emotions are a hindrance to the decision-making process. They may be quite oblivious to the feelings of other people. The F may be motivated not to cause distress or hurt to other people.

They both consider themselves to be correct in their respective decisions because they are looking at the question from different viewpoints. Any concern from the T is likely to be *sympathy*, whereas from the F it would probably be *empathy*. The approach of T is one of detachment (outside of the 'self'), while F is letting the heart rule the head.

3 The person who engages in sensing (S) is taking in the objective world through perceptual processes, through the senses. When finding out information or making decisions they tend to be practical, observant, skilful in remembering facts and processing them.

4 The person who engages in (N) is relating to experience that cannot be articulated and relies on *imagination*, constantly on the lookout for fresh ideas and stimulating projects.

The S is a methodical person who pays attention to detail and is good at tasks involving repetition. The (N) essentially likes variety and new and different experiences, and will work on many different jobs all at once.

'The big five'

We all exhibit specific traits – from the many hundreds that there are – which, when split up into clusters, or groups that go together, give an indication of our personality type. These traits can be grouped together into a number of major categories. These are the five to ten traits that together best describe an individual's personality. In recent years research has identified what are now known as the 'big five' dimensions of personality:

1 *Extraversion*
   Qualities exhibited: sociable, affectionate, fun-loving, adventurous; at the other end of the scale: reserved, aloof, sober, quiet.

2 *Openness*
   Qualities exhibited: imaginative, sensitive, creative; at the other end of the scale: down to earth, crude, insensitive.

3 *Agreeableness*
   Qualities exhibited: gentle, trusting, forgiving, good-

natured, helpful; at the other end of the scale: irritable, ruthless, manipulative, suspicious, uncooperative.

4 *Conscientiousness*
   Qualities exhibited: well organised, hard working, ambitious, precise; at the other end of the scale: careless, weak-willed, negligent, unreliable.

5 *Emotional stability*
   Qualities exhibited: calm, unemotional, poised; at the other end of the scale: nervous, hypochondriacal, emotional, anxious.

These five dimensions are quite basic and many personality psychologists are of the opinion that five dimensions are inadequate to embrace the individual nuances of personality. Nevertheless, they are useful for making quick assessments of personality.

A number of studies have been carried out whereby researchers arranged for strangers to meet and interact briefly and then rate each other according to the 'big five'. A comparison was made with the ratings given by relatives and friends of the respective individuals and there was a lot of agreement with many of the results on certain dimensions within the five. The two that stand out time and time again in terms of accuracy are extraversion and conscientiousness.

It has been shown that a person's personality type is closely linked to their work performance. For instance, studies consistently prove that people classified in the conscientiousness dimension perform well in all jobs. Being self-disciplined and organised, they are good time-keepers and can be relied upon to get things done on time.

For people in sales and management jobs, the dimension of extraversion is shown to be important. This fits in with the general consensus that successful sales people are sociable and person-oriented, not being afraid of interacting with new people all the time. They need to have a high sensitivity to others.

As regards the dimensions of agreeableness and emotional stability, people working in customer-service jobs fit into this category and show a high degree of success within that type of employment. Those who score in the agreeableness category tend to be easy to get along with and trusting and those in the emotional stability category are able to cope with high stress levels; you will typically find them in jobs that require calm under pressure.

We're all a *blend* of different types, but when it comes to clients, employers, etc., there are some real sterotypes that you will come across in your daily professional life. Identifying them allows you to adopt the appropriate techniques for handling them. You've almost certainly met some or all of the following types.

(Note: although 'he' and 'his' are used throughout, the traits illustrated can obviously be displayed by both men *and* women. Similarly, the secretary/assistant may equally well be male or female.)

'Get on with it – give me the bottom line'

Not too difficult to fix up a meeting

This type is willing to give most people a chance if he approves of their initial approach. Somebody who didn't waste too much of his time on the telephone, for instance, would probably be granted a meeting (you may have telephoned this person about a possible job vacancy or you may want to discuss your product or service).

This type likes to keep up with what's going on. If it's a possible 'superstar' job applicant or somebody that is offering a new product, he doesn't want to miss out to the competition; he doesn't want to be left behind. This makes him want to know more.

Talks quickly

This is symptomatic of the rest of his personality. *Time* is constantly on his mind. In fact, he probably looks at his watch at regular intervals while talking to you. He doesn't make any attempt to do it surreptitiously; he's blatant about it. *His* time is being spent; *yours* doesn't enter into the equation.

For this type of person, time is money. 'I can't spend too much time . . .' is one of his frequent sayings. His secretary judges the status of his visitors by how much time he spends with them. Time is the measure of success.

Coffee comes within three minutes

It's been ordered well in advance and brought in by a secretary with an endless smile. He probably has his own mug with some sort of inscription on it (ego-boosting), bought for him by someone in the office as a present – and a dig!

If you finish your coffee in the first five to ten minutes, it's easier to get thrown out; so take your time. If he turns out to be only half-interested, or has lost the gist of the conversation because of interruptions, he may well grant you only as much time as it takes to drink your coffee. It gives him an indication of the earliest point at which he can terminate the meeting. You need time to bring him back on the right track. *It*

wasn't your fault there were interruptions. So take it slowly and keep the coffee cup within his line of vision.

You can unnerve this type if he thinks that you have temporary control over the proceedings. If you want to stay (and you've finished your beverage) then sip *imaginary* mouthfuls from your cup (like they do in the 'soaps').

Studies you intently

He maintains a steely eye contact with you (when not looking at his Rolex) while you're speaking. He's listening only for key words that might be of interest. The rest of the time he's checking you out: clothes and body language – speech, mannerisms, signs of nervousness.

Desk shows a lot of activity

Because he likes to be in on the action, his desk is covered with a lot of visual 'noise' (that's why he'll sometimes meet you in the boardroom or one of the meeting rooms). Small wonder he doesn't like wasting time. If he sat around seeing people like you all the time, he wouldn't be visible from your side of the desk.

Wants you to get to the point quickly

This is the essential hallmark of this type. He likes people who cut through the flannel and are succinct and sincere. He's worldly wise enough to know what is what, so he wants your message to be *straight*. If he senses waffle and double-speak he starts to show signs of impatience (his body language is easy to read as he doesn't try to supress it).

If that's allowed to happen, you're sunk. This type of person is thinking of a thousand things at once anyway; if you ramble on, he'll just switch on to some of the other 999.

Essentially, this type can be a blessing to deal with if your pitch is right, whether you're selling yourself for a job, or for a product or service that you're involved with. He will always want to buy *you* first; and if that hurdle is overcome, he will deal with you on his terms. The fact that you got to the 'bottom line' quickly indicates that you value your time too. He definitely appreciates this quality in others. You know where you stand with a person like this.

This type of person achieved his present position by sorting out the wheat from the chaff – and that includes the likes of you.

Aggressive: 'What's in it for me?'

Heavy security

You were probably subjected to the third degree before being able to fix up a meeting. You may have had the initial 'Can you write in?' from his secretary or assistant. But your persistence got you through to him, and he agreed to see you (under sufferance). He emphasised the fact that he couldn't promise anything.

You're guilty until proven innocent

With this type, you're observed suspiciously from the start. You're made to feel very much like an intruder when you enter his domain. This is designed to make you feel uncomfortable. He wants the upper hand. He'd like to see you crack. If you're seeing this person with some kind of business proposition this would mean you'd probably offer him a better deal, under pressure.

Knows all about you (or so he thinks)

He claims to know all about you (or your company) from his colleagues, previous dealings and other vague sources. He actually knows very little – but he has these set preconceived ideas. He therefore has a *listening* problem. He is reluctant to give the appropriate attention, and nods continuously to indicate 'Yes, I know. Yes, I know.'

It often turns out that he has confused your company with another. So all his criticism and negative views are wrongly directed at you. If you discover this during the meeting and point out the case of mistaken identity, you risk making him lose face. This type cannot cope with that (big ego). So you suffer because he couldn't be bothered to check his facts beforehand.

Suffers from desk aggression

Psychologists have long recognised the change that comes over certain people when they get behind the steering wheel of a car (the polite term 'road rage' is the common term these days). Otherwise thoughtful and kind human beings can become menacing and aggressive in these circumstances.

Put some people behind a large desk and you get an almost parallel situation; let's call it 'desk aggression'. It gives this

type a feeling of power and causes a personality change. The bigger the desk, the bigger the transformation that takes place.

Try to get this type *away* from his power base if there's alternative seating (your bad back, the need for a power point for your laptop – anything). It could alter the outcome of your meeting.

Looks for ways of tripping you up

Basically, he didn't really want to meet with you. But you persisted. So it's a case of: 'Come into my parlour for some Chinese torture.'

He'll try to catch you out in what you say. His ego tells him that whatever he is doing at the moment, he's doing it *right*. He doesn't need whatever you're offering. Why introduce another variable into the equation and upset the balance? He's thinking: 'What's in it for me? No thanks. I'll stick with who we've got at the moment. They're not brilliant, but who needs a change?'

Criticises features relating to your proposition

This type invariably finds fault with aspects of your proposition. It's easier that way. All the time there is an ego-based justification for sticking with the *status quo*, he will refuse to accept that the way he has been operating could be improved upon. So he goes through all the aspects of your proposal and demolishes them. Any valid resistance on your part to his claims is bulldozed.

This type will try to manipulate you from the word go. Keep your cool. He may make concessions if you can maintain your position. The fact that you've refused to budge too much indicates in his eyes that you've got something to offer. Now he's more interested.

General advice for tackling this type of person: *use your head* (and wear a crash helmet). Be prepared for a few knocks and don't take it personally. Be especially assertive.

Meticulous and methodical

Don't be a minute late

You're dealing with somebody whose life is highly organised. He may be an older person and may have been with the organisation for many years. He's very much 'dyed in the wool'.

When you fixed the meeting (for your job interview, presentation, etc.) he was very *specific* about time (11.40 am, for example) and probably insisted on giving you directions (even though you told him not to bother as you once worked opposite his offices – he just spoke over you and didn't listen). Just hear him out. If you don't you'll offend. His whole life revolves around *detail*; don't try and change it.

You're due at 11.40 and the meeting will certainly not last longer than forty minutes. At exactly 12.20 his secretary will come in, like clockwork, with his cup of tea and he'll be taking his cheese sandwich and chelsea bun out of his briefcase as he bids you goodbye.

Doesn't like people who talk fast

Slow down your speech with this type. Things have to be conducted at a certain pace – *his* pace. If you talk fast he thinks you're trying to gloss over certain points. This type is more comfortable with people who 'mirror' their verbal and non-verbal behaviour.

Long pauses when he talks to you

He's a cautious person generally, and this applies to his choice of words. Consequently he s-t-r-e-t-c-h-e-s everything out, and there are long pauses in mid-sentence. It's difficult to know when to start talking, because you don't know when he's finished discussing a particular point.

If you interrupt him inadvertently, he'll never forgive you. You think he's finished his sentence; then, just when you thought it was safe to go back into the conversation . . . !

'Just when you thought it was safe . . .'

Has done extensive research

It's a by-product of his nature that he has to have all relevant facts and assess all possible alternatives before making up his mind on anything.

In your case that means he's evaluated possible alternatives to your proposition; so you had better be clued up on what you're proposing. He won't tell you what his own research has shown him – on the contrary. That's one of the reasons why he s-t-r-e-t-c-h-e-s everything out; there's less chance of him accidentally giving anything away. He's researched other alternatives; he knows what else is on offer, and his filing cabinet will testify to that. He hoards information like a squirrel hoards nuts.

Wants straight answers

When he asks you a question, make sure you answer it (this is not the time to practise for a future in politics). His mind is programmed to receive a reply. Without one, the computer cannot go on to the next instruction.

Wants everything in writing

After the meeting he will insist that everything you've discussed be put in writing (hope you made lots of notes). This doesn't necessarily signal interest in your proposition. It is more of a safety valve (for him) should he actually decide to talk to you again.

Unfortunately, the lack of spontaneity in this type means that you rarely get any agreement at an initial meeting. Much of your face-to-face impact is lost because of having to go away and put everything discussed in writing. The sad thing is that this sort of person *forgets* most of the original discussion and remembers only what is said in the subsequent, often flavourless letter.

The matter is very much in his hands now. You can't force another meeting, and the best you can hope for is that you're contacted again. So your letter has to be effective. Reiterate the good points you made; don't dwell on his unfounded concerns. It's up to him to remember those. Cover most of the important points. Always remember that he's probably going to discuss this with somebody else in the organisation – and that person hasn't even seen you.

Calls you back to meet a third party

If he asks you back for another meeting, he will probably bring in somebody else. It may be a person who has a vested interest in your discussion. His instinct for playing safe means that he wants approval from the third party. Or, as is probably more often the case in job interviews and in business, he wants to be able to *dilute the blame* if things don't turn out quite right ('Well, John agreed we should hire him. He was also impressed with the guy's track record' 'Guy and Geoffrey thought the proposal was cost-effective compared to . . .').

Try to work out what type the third party is and handle

him accordingly. But remember that the ultimate decision-maker is your original contact Mr Methodical. Aim to get the third party to influence him. Let *him* take the reins.

Remember that essentially you're dealing with a *pedant* here. If you can recognise this difficult type and have the patience and understanding to cope with him, you can get results. But make sure your proposition is sound. This type can be a pain if there is cause for complaint. Have your air ticket and passport ready!

Friendly: 'I'll talk to anybody'

Very receptive to your phone call

When you first telephone, he's quite easygoing and pays attention to what you say. If he's interested, he sells *you* the idea of a meeting between the two of you. (Makes a nice change.)

Calls you by first name on arrival

He disposes of formalities and, being the friendly sort, immediately calls you by your first name (he may have worked in the US or have close links there by virtue of the organisation he works for). He perhaps asks you to call him Tom, Dick or whatever.

Has an unconventional seating arrangement in his office

His office is very homely; it's an extension of him. His desk, and its immediate surrounding area, is intended for his use only; it is tucked away at the far corner of the room. He doesn't like discussions from his desk; it's too territorial, and not fair on his visitors. Besides, the papers and clutter would prevent him from giving undivided attention to you. This is a godsend for you. You may sit on a couch or comfortable chair

– it's all very *relaxed*. 'Take your jacket off, if you like,' he offers.

Talks a lot initially

When you first meet, he talks a lot to put you at ease (very common with good interviewers who are assessing job applicants). He speaks with animated gestures and facial expressions that say 'I'm enjoying life' and also 'I'm enjoying our conversation' (although you haven't said anything yet!).

Asks you about your personal life

This guy just shows a keen friendly interest in you. He's *a people person*; he makes no bones about it – he's got good 'people skills' and you're going to benefit from this. His experience tells him that you're a nice person to deal with (whatever the outcome), so he's finding out more about you. He asks about your hobbies and interests (which you may touch upon quite naturally in the conversation, when you notice his rugby trophy, for example) and looks for common ground. He may leave discussion about what you actually came to see him for (!) till much later.

Agrees to your proposition quickly

If he's interested, he likes to tell you so almost immediately: he doesn't believe in playing games once he's made up his mind, one way or the other. You've passed the test. You're on to the next stage with him now and he wants to know what that is. He values *your* time as well as his own.

It's bound to be a pleasure dealing with a person of this type. He invites empathy and sincerity (he shows it himself), and if you've got it, you can hardly fail. He is undoubtedly the *ideal* type to deal with. There are a few of them around, but they're not that easy to find.

Amicable: 'Let's get you off your guard'

There is a variation on the friendly type that is worth mentioning. His friendliness is motivated by *self-interest* – he wants to lull you into revealing information.

Pleasant welcome when you arrive

You are greeted by your first name and made to feel like a long-lost friend.

Seating is informal

Similar to the previous type.

Keen to know your 'status'

If you're seeing this person on a business matter he will study your business card closely; he wants to gauge your seniority. He asks how long you've been with your organisation (or had your own company or whatever). He wants to know whether you have the clout to make a decision on a deal (that he's carefully thought out before you arrived) or whether you'd have to get approval from someone else back at the office.

If he works out that you do have ultimate authority, as well as coffee you'll be offered biscuits!

By establishing your track record, he may just be ensuring that he's dealing with someone experienced. That's quite in order. So he's checking out your credentials, and if he's not happy, you may have a very short meeting. ('What? He's only been in the business for three months? I've been in it twenty-eight years; he can't tell me anything. I'll cancel the coffee. Now, where's that ejector-seat button?')

If you feel that your short career within your present organisation may make him uneasy, in terms of his confidence in you, make sure you allude to your previous experience.

Tries to make you feel relaxed and off guard

This type knows that in most formal situations where you are visiting somebody (it can even be another person's office in the same building in which you work), it is the host who has the territorial advantage.

So by departing from the norm and making you feel relaxed and open in conversation, he's likely to get a little more out of you – maybe a *lot* more. Who knows, you may even tell him some secrets (office gossip, competitor information). But he could just be testing you. If you reveal things about *them*, you may reveal things about *him*! ('Thanks for the useful information; it'll come in very handy. And by the way – I'm sorry I can't help you.')

This friendly type also knows that if you are relaxed, you're likely to compromise that bit more in a negotiating situation. After all, if the visitor is made to feel well-received, he'll probably make an extra effort.

This type is *calculating*. So make sure that, despite the relaxed surroundings, you remain totally in control. He's hoping to put you in an expansive mood. If you falter at all,

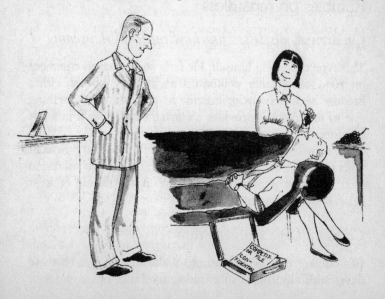

he'll seize on this as a chance to take advantage. Remain alert. If he agrees to your proposition and you bend a little to make it more attractive to him, let him see it's a *deliberate* decision on your part, and not the result of weakening under pressure. He'd rather deal with somebody strong-minded.

Most people are a cocktail of different personality types, but certain traits seem to form in 'clusters', as we noted at the beginning of the chapter. Understanding different behavioural features and mentally classifying those so afflicted (or blessed!) will be an enormous aid in using your ESP techniques.

With most types, there is a little bit of another type trying to get out. You can draw this out by your line of questioning. But the techniques you use will also depend on what type you are.

What type are you?

How do *you* come over to other people? In other words, what type are you? Let's take a look at a few examples:

Rambles on regardless

On arrival, discusses journey/traffic ad nauseam

This type can't help himself. He feels compelled to comment on road or weather conditions as an easy opener, either because he is nervous or because he can't think of anything else to say. Also, it provides a convenient opener if he's not comfortable being there.

Of course, it's all right to remark on the ups and downs of your journey, your parking problems and rail cancellations; in fact, the other person may even ask. But it should be kept *brief*. It isn't the point of the visit.

Carries a large synthetic case

His bulging case is off-putting. We're into high tech these days, with electronics substituting for bulk. His case looks like its just come off the baggage reclaim carousel. It contains masses of literature, case studies, personnel files, biros, a shoe horn and so on. The sight of this can be an immediate turn-off to the other person, who doesn't want a hard time – he's got time constraints, like everybody else. What's going to come out of this Pandora's Box?

Floods the person's desk with papers

He assumes the other person is a graduate of the rapid reading school and starts by overloading him with visual material. He's latched on to that old favourite: 'A picture paints a thousand words.' He doesn't understand about timing and relevance.

Talks while the other person is trying to read

Ugh! It's bad enough for the poor person struggling with the heaps of paper put in front of him. As he tries to read, his visitor is wittering away. He doesn't know what to concentrate on. Should he be listening and looking at his visitor, or should he be reading? He can't do both. There is no answer to this one.

Pays no regard to time

This type doesn't attempt to find out how much time the other person has before his next engagement. He rambles on regardless, intent only on the time he has to kill ('I'll stay till it stops raining . . . till the parking meter runs out . . . till 2.35, then I can catch the 3.10 . . .').

Monotonous and mean with words

Speaks in a monotone

This type is oblivious to the handicap of his dull speaking voice and goes through life inflicting misery on his listeners.

With no variation in his speech, he could win a Dalek contest. Because there is no enthusiasm in his voice, if he tries to sell himself or his ideas, he is doomed to alienate his audience. On the telephone, his monotone is magnified even more.

Uses a minimum of facial expressions

His face shows no warmth or sincerity; he rarely smiles. It never occurs to him. He sees work, and life itself, as a *serious* business. Since he displays scarcely any non-verbal signs of emotion, the other person never knows whether this type is on the same wavelength, or whether he cares and understands about his problems and requirements.

Speaks almost from a script

For some uncanny reason, the above type is usually guilty of further aggravating the situation by speaking in a stilted almost scripted way. You can imagine him at home saying to his wife: 'It's come to my attention, that the radiator in the back room is leaking.'

His complete lack of empathy, sincerity and perspicacity prevents him getting inside the other person's mind, identifying their type and tailoring his words accordingly. It's a script – delivered in that characterless voice. Could anything be worse?

He's done it so many times that it follows a set pattern. If the other person comes up with a question or argument that's not in the script, forget it. It's just edited out. There's no room for improvisation.

Often talks over the other person

Watching this happen is quite painful; and when you're on the receiving end, it really hurts. You may see it on TV chat shows and in other interview situations. Talking over the other person's words may be the stock in trade of politicians, but in everyday dealings it's very rude.

We are all guilty *occasionally* of talking at the same time as somebody else – in an argument, for example, or if we're excited about something. That's acceptable.

But it's not acceptable in a professional setting, when you're aiming to sell yourself. You need to know exactly what the other person is saying so that you can formulate a reply, quite apart from manners . The other person won't voice their disapproval (though their body language will give it away, if you're attuned to it); they'll probably just reject you.

Whatever they do in life, people of this type will find it very difficult to relate effectively on an interpersonal level or get their message across effectively. When they're trying to influence or persuade people to come round to their way of thinking, their chances of successs are very low.

Over-familiar, over the top

Uses first name too soon

This type calls the other person by his first name as soon as contact is made (often on the phone).

This issue needs to be addressed. Say you're telephoning a potential client, Nick Peters, for the first time. The secretary puts you through to her boss. If you begin by saying: 'Hi, Nick. It's Tom Smith from Universal Imports speaking' your forwardness is unlikely to be well received. It's different if you've been referred to Nick by a mutual friend or acquaintance you know fairly well, and they've suggested you call him (and may even have let Nick know to expect a call).

Many people object to over-familiarity. They might accept your using their first name at the end of conversation, when you've established rapport, but not while you're an unknown quantity. To many people it immediately spells insincerity. Whatever you say next may be lost.

The first-name approach is an accepted practice in the USA, and although it has gradually crept over to this side of the Atlantic, a traditional British reserve still dictates a certain protocol. So remain on a formal footing until you've built up some kind of empathy.

Flatters insincerely

There's nothing wrong with the odd compliment or piece of flattery – if it's meant sincerely.

If appropriate, it can be taken as a positive show of interest and set a pleasant mood to a discussion. Insincere flattery could have a much worse effect than labelling you as superficial. It can introduce doubt into the other person's mind: 'If you can flatter me, then you're probably flattering your CV/proposal/etc. So I don't trust you.'

Regards listening as time-wasting

This type goes on speaking without pausing for breath. He believes that silence is a void to be filled – by *him*, not by anybody else. After all, he's the one with the proposition, so he should do all the talking. Unfortunately, he's never listened long enough to learn the error of his ways.

Over-enthusiastic about his proposal

He refuses to believe or even consider that there are any possible negative points or flaws in his line of reasoning. He's so obsessed by the common directive to *be positive* (or the flip side – not to be negative) that he carries it too far. As far as he's concerned, what he's proposing is simply the best. He won't encourage a dialogue that might allow the other parties to voice any objections or concerns to have these laid to rest. He doesn't give them a chance to weigh things up.

Sulks visibly on rejection

When he's given a thumbs-down verdict, this type of person is mortified. ('What? You've made me speak non-stop for the last forty-five minutes for nothing? You cannot be serious!')

Instead of analysing the reasons for his non-convincing display, he may aggravate the situation by telling the other person that he 'drove two hours in the rain to get there'; 'is not impressed by their way of operating'; 'is convinced they're making a big mistake', etc. He thus ruins any chance of the door being left open for future contact.

People can change their minds at a later date. It's natural. We all do. Circumstances change. Life is not static. We may just have caught someone on a bad day.

If you've left the door open and parted amicably, then there may be another opportunity. If you challenge the other person's decision and react badly to losing out, you may burn your boats.

This type of person never establishes any degree of rapport with people generally, and certainly not with business contacts. If he's successful in reaching an agreement with someone, and things don't turn out to the other person's satisfaction, they will see the same inflexibility and insincerity they encountered (and excused) when they first met him. Result: loss of goodwill.

Confident and assertive: 'It's in your interest to talk to me'

Acknowledges that other people's time is precious

This type creates a good impression from the first minute by showing that he knows other people are busy.

Being inaccessible to all and sundry is equated with status. So when you acknowledge that somebody has *limited time*, you're saying between the lines: 'I know you're in demand, therefore I appreciate you taking time to talk to me (but it's worth it – otherwise I wouldn't be bothering you).' This implication makes the other person more amenable. He's a busy individual in an important position which affords him esteem. People respect him. They show that they they *appreciate* being given some of his time. (What would we do without ego?)

There is further prestige – for both parties – in letting the other person know that you are busy too. He wants to deal with other busy/successful people – like you. It makes you members of the same club. So let him know your time is valuable by taking the cue for leaving, don't outstay your welcome; tell him how much time you can spare. You're helping to shape his perspective of you.

Lets the other person pick the pleasantries

In our first dealings with people, we all need some warming up, rather like an athlete preparing for a performance. Your aim is to try and establish some empathy early on. It can be awkward for both parties when you haven't met before (first impressions), but it's a bit worse for you if you're visiting somebody on their home ground. It's a little easier in neutral surroundings.

So let the other person take the lead. If you end up talking about something which he is interested enough to prolong, and he's enjoying the discussion, fine. That's what you're there for anyway. To get inside his mind. To find out what makes him tick, what his interests are, and also his values. Everything follows from that. You know that very well from your own experience.

You're selling yourself as a good listener. People appreciate good listeners. Let him decide when to cut it short.

Makes the person feel comfortable

This is an extremely valuable quality. Most people's attitudes and reactions are shaped by the other person's demeanour. If you are tense, you may make the other person so. If you smile, you'll probably find it's contagious. You're trying to create the right mood, and you want them to be relaxed (because people give more of themselves when they feel this way), so be comfortable within yourself. Look as though you're bent on enjoying the meeting and want to help the other person. With a smile in your voice, you're letting them know that there's no compulsion to accept your message, so they needn't be on their guard. Remember, you're dealing in the art of gentle persuasion.

The other person may be a serious type and may need drawing out. They may just be worried, or in a bad mood for some reason. You need them to be in a receptive frame of mind. People will, all things being equal, generally mirror your mood after a while. If the person sitting opposite you is being pleasant, for example, it's hard not to be pleasant back. Be patient. Try it.

Maintains eye contact most of the time

This type of person reads body language well and picks up all the signals. The point is often laboured, but successful negotiators in all walks of life will testify to the fact that the eyes can reveal all.

Watch the eyes the next time you're talking to somebody. When you ask a question and are given a verbal answer, look for the eye message too. We often say one thing and then provide a supplementary answer with our eyes. It can be a valuable way of finding out what somebody is really thinking.

Sincerity shows in our eyes when we feel strongly about something. Similarly, if we're lying or being insincere, an astute person can pick this up.

Maintaining eye contact shows that we are listening. This gives more depth to the conversation. If we look interested, the other person's interest is sustained. Looking somebody squarely in the eye gives the impression that we're being 'up front'.

Spectacle wearers can have a problem here, incidentally. Light reflected on their lenses (if they haven't been coated) means that the person looking at them may see only rays of light. This is not very helpful for making and maintaining eye contact, and it can be off-putting. Similarly, heavily tinted or dark glasses prevent eye messages being sent (or picked up). Making – and keeping – eye contanct becomes virtually impossible.

10

Negotiating to resolve and to win

Every day of our lives we spend a lot of time negotiating, even though we're quite unaware that we're doing so. Because much of it happens informally, we may not realise any negotiation has taken place

We may think of negotiation as something we read about in papers and see on the nine o'clock news, but it's much more than that. In our interpersonal dealings we are arch negotiators. We negotiate over our pay increases, we jointly decide which video to rent, what restaurant to eat in, who'll mow the lawn; we sell houses, buy cars, negotiate compensation for a faulty freezer. The list goes on and on.

Good negotiation skills are an asset because we are constantly having to negotiate. Like it or not, we are all *interdependent on each other*. We have interests that may differ from those of people we interact with. Result: conflict.

Negotiating to resolve conflict

A great deal of the negotiation we are forced to engage in, therefore derives from the following:

1 Our interests are incompatible with another person's interests.
2 Another person has interfered (or is intending to) with our interests.

Extensive research by social psychologists has shown that there are a number of different ways in which we respond to conflict, either in an everyday life situation or in a work setting. People will display one of the following five tendencies:

1 Competition: *try to get the maximum possible for themselves.*
2 Accommodation: *give up and let the other party have all the benefits.*
3 Compromise: *for example, split everything down the middle.*
4 Avoidance: *the desire to walk away from any kind of conflict.*
5 Collaboration: *a focus on maximising gains for all parties.*

Essentially, research has shown that two scenarios are created: first, there is a situation in which the goal relates to *our well-being*, and second, to the *well-being of others*. For example, accommodation is more concerned with others and less for ourselves; competition is more concerned with ourselves and less with others; compromise shows an equal preference.

What tactic is used is completely dependent upon the situation. But the most common method that we tend to adopt in problem-solving is one of negotiation, where the goal is to maximise joint benefit. Within ongoing relationships we obviously negotiate in a different fashion to the way we behave with strangers and acquaintances. After all, within personal relationships, or among work colleagues, there is an unwritten law that we care about one another's interests.

The key to good negotiation – and therefore problem-solving – is to indicate clearly *what you want*. We all have a right to certain wants, needs and goals. Equally, there are situations where others have the right to block you if what you want goes against their best interests. But you must at least communicate your desires.

The next step is listening – really listening – to the other person's wants. As a result, the conflict is defined as *a mutual problem that has to be solved*.

Both parties having stated what they want, they must now express how they *feel*. This is something that most people find difficult. You may be angry, exasperated, shocked, afraid. But it's very important to share your feelings. You can show anger without being aggressive, for example. Anger and aggression are not the same thing. The other person then knows the effect their actions are having on you.

Many conflicts are never properly resolved because true feelings were never disclosed. If anger is suppressed, because of a reluctance to disclose true feelings, and an agreement is made, then hostility may still remain and future dealings will suffer.

So having expressed your feelings, and the desire to solve the problem ('I'm confident we can work something out so that we're both satisfied'), you need to show that you can *both* achieve what you want. (Fact: for every need or want there are usually several options to satisfy it.)

We often assume that, because somebody takes a different line or position to our own in an interactive situation, their goals are also opposed to ours. This isn't always the case. There are often shared and mutual goals as well as some that differ. Work out the differences between your wants and goals and the other person's. Where are they the same? Take a look at your common and opposing interests. It is often by sacrificing some of the opposing ones that you can build on common concerns and needs.

You may then come up with a number of possible agreements to choose from to resolve the problem. The one that is fair to both and increases the likelihood of an amicable long-term relationship is ideal.

Negotiating to win

Problem: everybody wants to be the winner. Who wants to be the loser? There's no fun in losing. But what constitutes a 'win' is normally subjective: it's in the mind – *your* mind.

The game of negotiating to win differs from all other games. That's because we're looking for *two* winners.

The process of negotiation starts only when something has been agreed upon, in principle. You've made your case about your proposition or product or service; the other person is convinced and is in the right frame of mind to take it a stage further and accept – except for a few minor points.

What points? The obstacle could be trivial, as far as you're concerned. But it's significant in the other person's mind. *And that's what matters.*

It's a joy to watch professionals negotiating. Not just over products and services but in the world of social affairs. Government ministers, for instance, negotiate every day; they trade concessions with other parties. It's exactly the same negotiating process, with both sides gaining something.

But many people do not understand the reasoning behind the principles of negotiation. They forget that negotiation takes place *after* something has been agreed in principle. You may persuade a potential employer that you are perfect for the job – but fail to negotiate well on certain sticking points and so fail to get it. You may manage to reach agreement over the sale of your product or service, but then negotiate ineffectively and lose the deal. You can see then that the successful professional has to be master of the whole process.

The plain truth is that the majority are poor negotiators. An understanding of the psychology behind negotiation can really improve results. Let's define the scenario:

1 You know that the other person wants a better deal.
2 Equally, they know that you want a good deal.

Who budges?

No one can be blamed for asking for a better deal ('I'd only consider it if there were six weeks' paid holiday.' 'Well, if you'll throw in the security system and air-conditioning, I may pay the figure you quoted.' 'You'd have to include free after-sales service for all our sites if we're to agree to the costs outlined.')

There never was a truer maxim than: 'If you don't ask, you don't get'. But just because somebody asks for something, it doesn't mean it has to be given. If it's reasonable and settles things without too much aggravation, monetary sacrifice (if relevant), or bad feeling, fine. But if both parties are dissatisfied, the equation is not right. Remember – it's a game with two winners.

If one half of the negotiating equation is not happy, the situation is also unsatisfactory. In any relationship, whether it be personal or workplace-related, if only one of the parties wins, the *relationship* loses. The aim is to satisfy the needs of both sides of the relationship to secure a win–win situation.

Consider these points:

1 An unhappy customer is not likely to buy from you again (and may pick faults with your product or service after delivery – and possibly withhold payment).

2 Equally, an unhappy supplier of goods or services is unlikely to give good service during and after the sale. The customer wanted the concessions, but not at the expense of something else. That wasn't part of the scenario.

Making concessions

Since negotiation is essentially a trading of concessions, we're looking for an *amicable compromise*. Most commercial transactions today require some element of negotiation. Very few are: 'Yes, I'll take it.'

Fact: as consumers (and in the corporate world) we're not always concerned about better price, delivery or payment terms and so on. We don't like being *sold to*: we'd much prefer to *buy* (i.e., retain control). Therefore, if we win concessions from the other person (on price, for instance) we feel we have bought, rather than having been sold to (ego). In effect, there's been a reversal of roles; we've 'sold' to the provider of the product or service (so we, the customer, feel as though we've won. Now, *there's* a switch!

Have certain concessions up your sleeve which if need be, you can bring into play. And perhaps a major concession which you can be flexible about. But don't offer them all immediately: leave something in the hat after the rabbit's been pulled out.

Game plan

The other person's problem: 'I don't know what your bottom line is. I don't know how much you are willing to spend, or what you'll settle for ultimately. So I want you to make the first move.'

Your problem: 'I don't know how far I can push you on price, delivery or payment. So we'll play ping-pong until someone digs in his heels and refuses to budge. If that's me, you make the concession.'

You're treading a thin line all the time. If your original demand is too high, you turn off the other person and don't even get to the negotiation stage. And yet you've got to give yourself room to manoeuvre. If you give your bottom-line figure immediately, with no concessions (because you've already included your concessions in the 'package'), the other person won't feel they were ever in the match, let alone that they've won.

It's tough psychologically because you don't want to alienate the other person. After all, they're in the right frame of mind for accepting your proposition; it's just these concessions that they're seeking.

If you watch the pros negotiating (at wage tribunals, economic summits, in the boardroom, etc.) you'll notice how they let the body signal their response to a demand. You'll see them shaking their head, smiling, flicking an imaginary speck of fluff of the tie or jacket, or giving occasional outbursts of laughter in disbelief. They're trying to let the other person know, without actually saying no, that the request is over the top. It's less offensive using body language.

The other person doesn't know whether what they've asked for is fair, and they're being given the signal that their *reasoning* is wrong. They may not seriously expect to get the concession – but they need to know how close they can get to it.

Getting inside the other person's mind is crucial here, as the other person's ego demands have to be met. If you can work out in what area their principal needs and fears lie, it will help you to decide which bait you need to use and how far you have to spread the net. They might be worried that a delivery let-down could lead to their own client raising a claim against them. In this case, you could offer to send the goods by overnight air freight at your expense. This would save eight days. They buy peace of mind from you: *a small concession for you, a big one for them.* Deal done.

Generally, you'll be pushed (or only allow yourself to be pushed) up to the limit of the concessions you're able to authorise. The other person can usually sense this from your own hesitancy and body signals. If they want more, you may have to consult with somebody. This can be an advantage and a disadvantage.

The advantage is that you are out of deadlock and have breathing space to check and see if ther's anything *else* you can offer that can ease the situation. And of course you can actually consult with other relevant people to see if you can go further (that's if you want to).

The disadvantage is that you've perhaps worked hard at building up momentum towards acceptance of your proposition during the face-to-face meeting and interest is running high (remember the attention curve?). Now you go away. This can change things. Say the person you are dealing with doesn't have a particularly good memory; they forget all the good points that they were so excited about at the first meeting. It's natural. So many things have happened since then: the roof fell in; they fell out with their boss; their company's lost a big contract; their health isn't good.

Their interest is not running so high. That's natural. You probably need to go through the whole process again. But they're too busy to see you now. They may even have seen somebody else offering something similar and agreed to this rival proposal on the spot. Timing is all-important.

Concluding

If you want to avoid reaching stalemate and losing momentum by leaving to check certain facts, you should wind up the process. Produce the ace up your sleeve:

'OK, then. If we get the celebration concert CDs to you already packaged with your logo printed, and we do it within three weeks – at no extra charge – is that a deal?'

'You're on.'

You should emulate a lawyer summing up at the end of a courtroom hearing at this final stage. The trick is to *restate what you're actually giving.*

During this inner game, people get so obsessed with the play in progress that *they forget what they've asked for.*

Analysis: by restating what you have just conceded to the other party, you are psychologically affirming what a good deal *they* have managed to get out of *you.* Game, set and match to *them*!

(Or is it to you both?)

11

All the world's a stage: acting the part

All the world's a stage,
And all the men and women merely players;
They have their exits and their entrances;
And one man in his time plays many parts.

William Shakespeare,
As You Like It (Act II, Scene vii)

Well, Shakespeare certainly got it right all those years ago. We're all like actors on a stage, seeking applause and the social approval that accompanies successful performances.

Our public self is motivated to gain the approval of others as we present our 'lines' to one another. Just like an actor who has to 'get inside the mind' of the role he is playing in front of his theatre audience, we try to portray our 'selves' in a certain way for the audiences that we encounter in everyday life.

Let's think about everything we've discussed so far in the book and how it relates to self-presentation. We'll follow the fortunes of Anthony Bates as he attempts to arrange a meeting. First, we'll look at how *not* to do it – the 'wrong' way – and then we'll look at the successful method – the 'right' way.

Dealing with the secretary

1   'Mr Saxby's office.'
        'Hello. I'd like to talk to Mr Saxby.'
        'Who's calling him?'
        'It's Anthony Bates, from Top Notch Hotels.'
        'May I ask what it's to do with?'

'It's something I'd like to discuss with him.'

'Has he spoken to you before, Mr Bates?'

'No, he hasn't.'

'Just a moment.'

'I've had a word with Mr Saxby. Could you tell me what it's all about?'

'Well, OK then. I wanted to come and see him about a new five-star property of ours.'

'One moment . . .'

'I've had another word with him. He's in a meeting, and he's rather tied up. He said if you'd like to write in he'll get in touch if he's interested.'

'No, you don't understand. I'm only over for a few days. I have to speak to him. I can't put anything in the post.'

'I'm sorry but he's very busy.'

'So am I!' *(Click)*

2 'Could you give me the name of Mr Saxby's secretary, please?'

'Yes – it's Anne Sims.'

'Would you put me through to her?'

'Putting you through.'

'Mr Saxby's office.'

'Yes, hello. Could I speak to Anne Sims, please?'

'Speaking.'

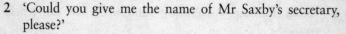

'Miss Sims – good morning. Can you help me? The name's Bates.' *(Pause)* 'My company is Top Notch Hotels. I'd like a quick word with Mr Saxby if he's available now.'

'Well, I know he's rather tied up now. I'll see. Does he know what it's concerning?'

'He probably knows my company. Would you tell him it's about a new five-star property of ours which I think he'd want to hear about? If he's busy now, perhaps you could ask him when I might have a few words with him.'

'Just a second, Mr Bates. Would you mind holding?'

'No – take your time, Miss Sims.'

'Mr Bates, he said he'll be free in around half an hour. If you leave your number he'll call you back.'

'No, that's OK. I'll call back in about forty-five minutes.'

'Very well.'

'Thank you. Bye for now.'

After forty-five minutes:

'Mr Saxby's office.'

'Is Anne Sims there?'

'Speaking. Is that Mr Bates?'

'Yes. Hello again.'

'Putting you through now.' *(Click)*

'Richard Saxby speaking.'

Arranging a meeting

1   'Good morning. Advertising Solutions. How can I help you?'

'Good morning. Could you tell me who's handling conferences now?'

'I'm not sure. I'm a temp here. I'll see if I can find out . . . Just a moment . . . let's have a l-o-o-k at t-h-i-s list . . . Oh, I'll just take this other call . . . Now, where . . . conf– . Just a moment . . . Sorry, I'm back. Could you hold on a minute?'

'Yes.'

Three minutes of piped music later:

'I've been through to Customer Service. They said it depends.'

'Depends on what?'

'Oh, I don't know really.'

'Look, just put me through to them.'

'Hold on.'

Two minutes later:

'I've spoken to them again. They said they think it would be Mr Steed. I'll connect you to his secretary. I'm not sure whether she's in yet.' *(Click)*

'Steed speaking.' *(Hurried and impatient voice)*

'Ah, Mr Steed. I'm through to you. Anthony Bates of Top Notch Hotels here. We've got a new five-star property with wonderful conference facilities. We've had lots of interest from companies like yours that arrange film screenings and celebrity dinners. I'd like to come and see you. Now would Tuesday at 9.15 be OK or would Thursday at 2.30 suit you better?'

'Well – neither, really.'

'Sorry – what do you mean?'

'Well, Mr Notch, what is it exactly you wanted to talk to me about?'

'As I said. Our new hotel.'

'What's the company again, Mr Notch?'

'It's Top Notch Hotels. Actually my name's Bates – Anthony Bates.'

'Right. Sorry, Mr . . . er . . . Bates. I'm in the middle of a meeting right now. My secretary's not in yet. Give me your number.'

'My number . . . Er . . . It's 0768 0432561.'

'I'll call you back in about fifteen minutes. Goodbye, Mr Notch.'

Two hours later, and still no call.

2   'Good morning. Advertising Solutions. How can I help you?'

'Morning. You *could* help me by telling me who handles conferences these days.'

'I'll just check for you. Could you hold for a moment?'

'Certainly. Thank you.'

'I've spoken to Customer Services. They said it depends on what it's to do with.'

'Right. I understand. Could you put me through to them, please? It's probably easier that way.'

'Yes. Who shall I say is calling?'

'My name's Bates.'

'Trying to connect you, Mr Bates.'

'Customer Services, Emily Peel speaking. Is that Mr Bates?'

'Yes. Good morning. I just need to know who's now responsible for organising conferences.'

'Certainly. That's Mr Steed. Is there anything I could help with?'

'Well, I'd like to have a *brief* word with Mr Steed, if he's available, about our new hotel; I'm only over for a short time as I'm based at our head office in Monte Carlo.'

'Would you like me to put you through to his secretary?'

'That would be good, Mrs Peel. Thank you.'

'Let me see if she's there.' *(Click)* 'Mr Bates, she doesn't seem to be answering. I'll put you through directly to Mr Steed's extension.'

'Steed speaking.'

'Mr Steed. I've just been speaking to Mrs Peel – she's just transferred me to you. My company's Top Notch Hotels.' *(Pause)* 'My name's Bates – Anthony Bates.' *(Pause)* 'Is it convenient to talk?'

'Well, actually I'm with somebody at the moment. But go ahead. what's it about?'

'Oh – I've called at an inconvenient time. Can I call you later, when you're free? I'd rather do that.'

'Very well. I should be free at around 11.30.'

'OK. I'll call then.'

'Sorry, what was your name again?'

'The company's Top Notch Hotels. My name's Bates.'

'Right. I'll speak to you later, Mr Bates.'

'Bye.'

At 11.35:

'Mr Steed. It's Anthony Bates here. I called you an hour ago.'

'Yes, Mr Bates. Top Notch Hotels, isn't it? What can I do for you?'

'Well, we have a new five star hotel in Cannes which might be of interest to you. It would be helpful if I can fix up a brief meeting with you.'

'When would you like to come? I'm up to my eyes in it this week, really.'

'Well, to be specific, as I'm only over for a few days, I wondered whether there might be a chance of, say, Tuesday at around 9.15? Or, if that's awkward, Thursday afternoon?'

'Thursday would be better. Would 2.30 be OK?'

'Yes. Can we make it 2.30 to 2.45, just in case I have parking problems?'

'That's fine. But you can use our car park at the back. Just give my name.'

'Thank you. See you then.'

'Goodbye, Mr Bates.'

A meeting (the first of three)

1   (*To receptionist*) 'Morning. I'm seeing Mr Burns at 11.45.'
   'Your name, sir?'
   'Anthony Bates. Top Notch Hotels.'
   'Would you take a seat?'

After some time, he is led to an office:

'Good morning, Mr Burns.'
   'Good morning, Mr . . . er, Mr . . .'
   'Bates.'
   'Yes. Sorry to keep you waiting out there.'
   'That's OK.' *(He sits down)* 'It's a pleasure to meet you. It's good of you to see me, especially after the last fiasco at the conference you held at our Gstaad hotel. I hope your clients were not *too* annoyed. Must be a couple of years now. I heard about it at one of our regional meetings.'
   'Now, what "fiasco" was that Mr Bates?'
   'Oh – you know. We dealt with your predecessor, Mr

Flint. The audio-visual company we'd arranged for you didn't turn up. Something to do with them losing paperwork that our offices had faxed to them. Some mix-up anyway.'

'I see.' *(Puzzled look. His mind is distracted now. He's intrigued to discover more about the previous dealings with this company that had let them down.)*

'Now, Mr Burns. I wanted to talk to you about our new property in Cannes. It has excellent conference facilities, three gourmet restaurants and a top-of-the-range health spa.' *(Reaches for his case and rummages around for several minutes. In the meantime Mr Burns decides to make a call.)*

'Gary – hello, it's John Burns here. I have a gentleman from Top Notch hotels here with me . . . Yes, that's right. Oh . . . sure, I understand. Yes. Oh, *did* they? Bye for now.'

'Here, I've got some floor plans and sample menus. This shows you the exterior of . . .'

(Burns glances at what is handed to him but is clearly detached from the proceedings.)

'What are the delegate rates mid-July, for around two hundred or so?'

'Well, that would be high season, so let's see what we could do if . . .' *(The calculator comes out and there is a long session of key-punching. Mr Burns' attention is drawn back to the pile of files on his desk and anxiety starts to creep in as he surveys the debris on his desk.)* 'Let me just give you this sheet here. I've scribbled down the reductions you would get if you switched from deluxe rooms to standard and also there's some different meal plans there.'

'Thank you, Mr Bates. Now, if you'll excuse me I've got some pressing work that I've just got to get finished. Thank you for coming to see me. I'll bear you in mind.'

'Oh, it's my pleasure. As I said, it's nice to make contact with your company again after the last unfortunate mess-up. Can I give you a call next week to see if we can arrange something?'

'No, don't bother. I mean – I'll get in touch with you if I'm interested.'

'Bye for now.'

Mr Burns is left thinking: 'I'm certainly not dealing with *them*. They may let us down again. Good job he told me about it – I'd never have known. Before my time. That wouldn't go down well with the boss. Anyway, at those rates, who needs to take a chance with someone new? I'm still on my trial period here. What a waste of time that was!'

As Anthony Bates gets into the taxi he thinks to himself: 'That went well. I'm sure that won't turn out to be a waste of time!'

2 'Good morning.' (Hands over a business card to the receptionist.) 'I'm seeing Mr Burns at 11.45.'

'Would you take a seat?' *(Receptionist walks away with his card and returns shortly to accompany him to the office.)*

'Good morning, Mr Burns.'

'Good morning, Mr Bates. Do sit down.' *(Burns studies the business card.)* 'I see you're based in Monte Carlo. Good weather there now. Better than ours, I suspect.'

'Just a little!'

'What have you got to tell me? Anything interesting?'

'Well, yes. Very, I hope. It's a new property we've acquired and completely refurbished in Cannes. Here's a brochure to give you an idea. You're still organising overseas conferences for clients, I understand.'

'Oh yes, very much so. We're using a lot of your competitors, as I'm sure you know. I've only been here two months now. I'm working on the programme for late 2001–2002. So your timing's good.'

'I see.'

'I'll probably be interested in your other properties in other destinations, but tell me about this new five-star in Cannes. What's a typical rate based on three to four hundred in September/October, which is something I've got to put together shortly?'

'Well, it will naturally vary according to the split of rooms you take. I've got a write-up on the hotel that was done last month. Perhaps you'd just like to have a quick look while I tot up some figures.' *(Bates does some scribbling while Burns is reading the article.)*

'Very impressive, Mr Bates. Have you got a rough idea of the figures?'

'Yes. Here they are. *(Bates passes him a piece of paper.)*

'Does that figure include VAT, Mr Bates?'

'Yes, it does. We would also include various day excursions for the spouses or whoever to various attractions at no charge, every day.'

'I think we can work together on this one, Mr Bates.'

'What would you like me to do next, Mr Burns?'

'I'll fax you details on Friday. It's quite pressing on the schedule so I need to tie it up. It's been at the back of my mind for ages.'

'We'll be pleased to fix it all up for you.'

'Your timing's good, Mr Bates!'

The second meeting

1 'Mr Peters will be with you in a moment. Perhaps you'd like to go on into his office and wait, Mr Bates?'

(Bates surveys the large office: an imposing circular table with three chairs; on the table, two half-full cups of coffee, a phone and a clean ashtray, numerous bookcases; at the far corner a large mahogany desk covered in papers. A large plaque adorning the wall catches his eye: 'I have known many troubles in my life. Fortunately they never happened'. He walks over to the desk, puts down his case and sits in the chair opposite it, removing a pair of gloves which are lying on the chair. After a few minutes, since nobody arrives, Bates walks over to the table, removes the ashtray and goes back to his seat. He lights a cigarette, putting the ashtray on the side of the desk.)

Two minutes later:

'Ah, Mr Bates. Apologies. I just had to get these letters. My secretary's off sick today.' *(He casts a sideways glance towards the circular table by the door and then walks over to Bates, shakes his outstretched hand, notices the burning cigarette in the ashtray and pointedly walks towards the window and opens it. He then takes his seat at the desk.)* 'Er . . . Can I remove this ashtray? Have you finished?'

'Oh yes, of course.'

'Now, Mr Bates. It's about three weeks since you called me. Can you brief me again? You were interested in telling us how you could help us with the anniversary celebrations that we're planning. Is that roughly it? I'll just sign these letters while you're talking.'

'Yes. We've got a brand new five-star property in Cannes and we have a ballroom that can accomodate up to 500 people. You mentioned on the phone that there would probably be 400–450 guests. Is that correct?' *(Silence, as Peters is studying and signing his letters, his head down.)*

'Sorry – er, is that correct?' *(Pause)*

'Is what correct?'

'I was saying that you mentioned 400–450 guests would be attending your anniversary.'

'Yes, about that.' *(He gets up, walks over to an out-tray, puts in the letters and then returns to his desk.)* 'Your rates are very expensive, aren't they, Mr Bates?'

(A knock on the door.) 'Excuse me, Mr Peters. Could you sign this petty cash voucher for the milk? Mr Mollet is in Cambridge today?'

'Let's have a look at this, Sarah. What's this? £3.42p, is it? I presume you've checked it's right, have you? Er . . . can somebody else not sign it?'

'There's nobody around, Mr Peters.'

'Oh, very well.' *(Glancing at Bates.)* 'Signing my life away again.' *(Sarah leaves.)* 'Now, where were we?'

'You were saying we were expensive.'

'Yes. We can get a good venue in France for less. What

else have you got to offer?' *(Bates takes out a large file and places it on the desk, covering a number of Mr Peters' papers. He takes out a loose leaf floor-plan and passes it to him. Mr Peters is concerned at the file that is covering his pristine sheets of paper. He keeps checking out the corner of his eye that they're not being mutilated. ('Should I ask him to move that heavy thing? No – I suppose I was blunt enough about the cigarette.') This is a great distraction for him. His concentration has gone. Then the telephone rings.)* 'Yes. OK, Richard. I'll stay on the line while you look for it.'

(Bates is staring directly at Peters and is showing, through the vernacular of the body, his impatience. Peters, sensing this, asks him to carry on talking and puts his hand over the mouthpiece.)

'So you see, Mr Peters even though . . .'

(Peters waves at Bates to stop talking as he resumes his phone conversation.) 'Yes. That's fine, Richard. We'll pick up on that later. Bye.' *(He shows signs of being preoccupied again as he loses eye contact)* 'Look, Mr Bates, leave that brochure of yours. I'll look through it when my secretary comes back. I'll ask her to put down our requirements and write to you. Now, have we got an address? Did you give me a card?'

'No, sorry. It slipped my mind. Here.'

'Oh. You're based in Monte Carlo. Tell me – that restaurant by the casino. Been there for years. Chap with a patch over his eye used to run it. Is it still there? Can't for the life of me remember the name. I used to go there regularly when I worked in Nice. Wish you'd have mentioned you were based there earlier. Liked to have had a chat. Anyway, must dash now – let me see you out.'

2   *(Bates walks into the office. The large desk by the window is covered in papers. The circular table looks a better bet. Peters obviously uses this area, as there are two half-empty cups left there. He sits down at the table. From his case he removes some papers.)*

'Mr Bates – apologies. I just had to get these letters off today. My secretary's sick.' *(They shake hands and Mr Peters sits down at the table.)*

'Mr Bates, it's three weeks since you telephoned me to arrange this meeting. Now, remind me about your proposition to do with our anniversary bash that we're planning. If you don't mind I'll just run through these letters for mistakes and then I can sign them. You carry on talking.'

'No, that's OK. You carry on with your letters while I get some paperwork together that I'd like to show you.' *(Bates finishes shuffling papers when he sees Peters return to the table after having deposited his letters in a tray.)* 'Right.' *(Bates hands over his business card; the other man reciprocates.)*

'Mmm . . .' *(Peters is studying Bates's card.)* 'You're based in Monte Carlo. I worked in Nice for a while, many years ago. I didn't know your group was owned by Sherwood Tuck Corporation.'

'Oh, yes. They bought us last year.'

'Do you know a chap called Scott Walker?'

'Yes. He's running North America now. He's President. Well, not *the* President!'

'No, quite. I worked with him about fifteen years ago in Florence. If you're talking to him, say hello from me.'

'Sure I will. Now, our new hotel in Cannes has a ballroom that caters for up to 500 guests or delegates.'

'What rate are we talking about here, roughly.'

'Well, we can base it on the type of room. . .'

(There's a knock on the door.) 'Excuse me, Mr Peters. Could you sign this petty cash voucher for the milk bill? Mr Mollet is in Cambridge today.'

'Let's have a look at this, Sarah. What's this? £3.42p, is it? I presume you've checked it's right. Have you a pen? Look . . . er . . . are you sure there's nobody else to sign it?'

'Nobody else is here Mr Peters.'

'Oh, very well.' *(Turns his gaze to Bates.)* 'Signing my life away again . . . Now where were we?'

'I'll just recap. I was saying that we can go up to 500

people in the new ballroom and your costs can come down substantially if you take a different spec of room to the deluxe. Here, let me show you a picture of the brand new standard rooms. They've got all the facilities' *(He stops talking while Peters studies the literature.)*

'These rates are a little bit higher than the proposal we got in for the hotel in Marbella. Would you be able to include transport from the airport within these rates?' *(Bates nods to show agreement. Then there is a telephone interruption.)*

'Sorry about that. What was I saying?'

'You were saying that you'd like us to include transport within the cost, which we'll be happy to do. I can guarantee that will be OK.'

'So what would that be for 460 guests roughly? It's that column here on the matrix. Is that right?'

'Yes. Do you want to take things a stage further?'

'Yes. I think, subject to a few nitty-gritty details which I'm sure we can sort out, we may be able to celebrate our important anniversary at *your* new hotel.'

'Yes, and if we make sure it's successful, which we'll aim to do, you can come back again 200 years later!'

'Well, you're a little younger than I am. I don't think I'll be able to make it!'

'I'll put some details to you in the post, urgently. And I won't forget to say hello to Scott for you.'

'And remind him he owes me five million lire – plus interest! Bye, Mr Bates.'

The third meeting

1   'Do come in, Mr Bates.'

'Thank you, Mr Hitchcock.'

'By the way, I'm sorry about last week. I know it was short notice, but it was unavoidable. These things happen, as you know.'

'What happened exactly?'

'You remember – I mentioned to you when I telephoned to cancel our meeting. I had a burst pipe at home; the whole house was flooded. I seem to recall you saying you had this problem last winter.'

'Did I mention that to you? Oh, yes . . . That's right.'

'Anyway, you've got some interesting overseas hotels, you said on the phone.' *(There is a knock on the door.)* 'Oh, Holly. Come in – sit down.'

'Thanks.'

'I'd like you to meet Mr Bates of Top Notch Hotels . . . Mr Bates, this is Holly Wood, our locations manager.'

'How do you do.' *(They shake hands.)*

'Mr Bates felt that their new-five star in Cannes and some of their other hotels around the world would be of interest to us in the coming year. Do you want to tell us a little more?'

'Sure.' *(Bates shows them various photographs.)* You'd be well taken care of with our DBC programme, so I'm sure you'll find there'll be no problem as other film clients that have been on DBC have been very pleased with the arrangement. In fact DBC offers more than . . .'

(Hitchcock is distracted; he's wondering what on earth DBC can be. He's nodding away but isn't really listening. He doesn't want to ask and appear ignorant – especially as Miss Wood doesn't appear to be showing any non-verbal signs that she might be having trouble with the jargon. He is now preoccupied with playing word games in his head in an effort to guess the answer. Mr Bates should have said what it is, he thinks. ('It's obviously significant. Still, never mind. I've missed most of what he's been saying now. I don't know how he expects me to be interested if he doesn't spell out essential details . . . Now where am I supposed to meet Eileen for lunch today?') Bates tries to reclaim Hitchcock's interest as he sees they've lost eye contact. But he can't grab his attention by using his name, because he's forgotten it. Now the telephone rings) 'Hitchcock speaking.' *(A blessing for Bates as he now knows his name, again.)* 'Yes, come up Beverley. I'm in the middle of a meeting but you may find it interesting.'

(Shortly afterwards, there is a knock on the door.) 'Come in, Beverley. Can I introduce you to Beverley Hills, Mr Bates. This is Mr Bates of Top Cat . . . sorry, Top Notch Hotels. He's come over to talk to us about some new properties. Grab a seat.'

(Bates promptly offers some of the paperwork to the new arrival. He then looks over to Hitchcock) 'What did you think of the comments relating to our superiority over similar venues in the area, Mr Hitchcock?'

'Well, it seemed to be very . . .' *(He hadn't paid attention.)*

'One-sided?'

'Well, I suppose you might say that. I feel that the hotel is more suited to . . .'

'Film companies with bigger budgets?'

'Well, maybe.'

'Yes, I thought you might say that. But with out of season rates tumbling, you'll find that they're very competitive for a hotel of this calibre.'

'Is it possible to have a . . . ?'

'Think about it?'

'Well, I was going to say, is it possible to have a look at that photograph again? But now that you mention it, perhaps we can put our heads together and we'll get back to you at some stage.'

'If you need any more information, please call me.'

'Yes. We know where you are.'

'Well, I hope you get your *roof* sorted out, Mr Hitchcock.'

'Er . . . I beg your pardon?'

'Your roof – hope it all works out.'

'Yes. Quite.'

When Bates leaves the three colleagues discuss his shortcomings:

'That fellow is worrying. Didn't ask any questions.'

'Didn't look you in the eye, either. He had no empathy for our particular needs. Was only interested in prattling on, even when I was trying to read his PR blurb.'

'Now, listen, Holly, you know about location hotels and all that. It's driving me crazy. *What the deuce is DBC?*'

'Pass!'

'Beverley? Come on – you *must* know!'

'Funny you should mention that. I've been dying to ask you two!'

2 'Do come in, Mr Bates.'

'Thank you, Mr Hitchcock.' *(Sits down as directed.)*

'Well, what happened with your burst pipe in the end? Was there much damage to your house?'

'Oh, that! Don't ask! The place is in an absolute mess. We can only use one room. My wife's still distraught. The insurance company have been in; they've given the go-ahead to get the repairs done immediately. I've just got to find some decent builders.'

'Oh, I am sorry. I sympathise with you, having had the same problem last winter, as I mentioned to you briefly on the phone.'

'Yes. Did you get your repairs done satisfactorily. Any problems?'

'No, it was relatively smooth. We found a very competent firm of builders. They're used to dealing with flood damage – they work really fast. As a matter of fact I think I've still got their number in my organiser here. If you're interested you could perhaps get an estimate.'

'That would be a great help. I'd really appreciate that.'

'Here it is. Noah's Construction Ltd. I'll just jot down their number for you.'

'Thank you. Now, we'd better get down to what's brought you here, or you'll be missing your plane! . . . We make films and television commercials, as you know, and in your original letter that you sent to me you mentioned a particular hotel of yours that might be suitable for some of our work.'

'Yes, I've seen the kind of work that you do. You tend to go for period-style properties don't you?'

'Well, we like to see what's around. We've just filmed around Dartmoor at The Manor House Hotel, a few miles from Exeter on the edge of the moor. Jacobean style property; stunning setting, lovely lakes and gardens, eighteen-hole championship golf course, you know the sort of thing. Used as Baskerville Hall for *The Hound of the Baskervilles* many years ago.'

'A lot of our places have superb settings. Just have a quick glance at this. This is our new property in Cannes.'

'Oh, Sandra . . . Coffee, Mr Bates? Right. Sandra, would you mind? Two coffees . . .'

'We get a lot of film crews staying at many of our hotels throughout the world. We're fortunate, I suppose, that they're mainly in superb settings. And they're predominantly older historic properties.'

'That's very interesting, Mr Bates. We've got a few things coming up – you've made me think. Oh, by the way, I've asked our locations manager to come and join us. She's got a few problems at the moment so she's in a bit of a tizz. You know how people let you down all the time. Let me try her line in case she's forgotten.' *(As he picks up the telephone theres a knock on the door.)* 'Come in. Ah, Holly, there you are. I was just ringing you. This is Anthony Bates of Top Notch Hotels. I mentioned him to you.'

'Hi. I'm Holly Wood. Nice to meet you.' *(They shake hands.)*

'Good to meet you. Sorry, I didn't quite catch your name – Holly . . . ?

'Wood. Holly Wood.'

'Right. Thank you'.

(They all sit down and Bates hands his business card to the new arrival.)

'Holly, Mr Bates was showing me particular hotels that might be good for some of our shoots. Perhaps you'd like to continue, Mr Bates. What were we saying?'

'You were telling me that you've got a few things coming up shortly we might be able to help you with.'

'Yes, that's right.'

(Bates hands a brochure and some photographs to each of them. When they have both finished reading and Bates can resume eye contact, he continues talking.) 'As you can see, as I mentioned to you earlier, Mr Hitchcock, they're historical properties and are popular with people in your line of work. During the low season, some film companies will take over the entire hotel and cast members and crew are resident there for long periods.'

'Yes. *I* wouldn't mind a long spell in those surroundings – eh, Holly?'

'And of course when you're with us in any of the hotels you're designated DBC clients. Since we've been running the DBC programme it's been a huge success. In fact DBC has resulted in us receiving an award last year, it was held in Hong Kong, and . . .' *(He notices by their body* *language signals that they're losing the thread.)* 'Oh, forgive me, I'm going on about DBC all the time, assuming it means something to you. It's our 'Doing the Best we Can' programme, which is a sort of VIP programme for preferred clients. We offer a whole lot of extras and guarantees of service and the scheme won us an award last year.'

'That's very good.'

'In fact there are a few paragraphs about it in this press-cutting here, if you'd like to take a look, Miss Wood?' *(He looks over to Mr Hitchcock while Miss Wood is reading.)* 'When you're shooting commercials, is there an average length of stay while you're away?'

'Well, as Holly will tell you, it can be anything from four days to a month.'

(Bates looks towards Hitchcock's colleague, who is engrossed in reading the press-cutting he handed her. *(She has seen something interesting on the same page: a recipe for 'the world's best sticky toffee pudding!'))*

'Is that right, Miss Wood?'

'Sorry, I'm getting carried away here, Mr Bates! I was just reading something else on this page. Very interesting.'

'Our hotels, or the sticky toffee pudding?'

'Both!'

'Mr Hitchcock was just telling me that when you're on location shooting commercials, the length of time varies a lot.'

'Yes, it sure does.'

(The telephone rings. Hitchcock answers it.) 'Yes, come up, Beverley. I'm in the middle of a meeting. You might like to meet the gentleman.'

(A few moments later there's a knock on the door.) 'Come in, Beverley. This is Mr Bates. He's from Top Notch Hotels. Beverley's our budgeting director on the film side, by the way.'

'Hello – I'm Beverley Hills.'

'Pleased to meet you, Miss Hills'.

'Let me see. Top Notch Hotels. Didn't I read something about you in *Film News* recently? Some award or something like that? Or maybe it was some other organisation.'

'That was us. Excellent memory, Miss Hills.'

'I remember it because it showed a picture of one of your hotels with the crew of *ESP – The Nightmare Begins* standing outside the front. A friend of mine is in that film.'

'I was showing Miss Wood a recent write-up of ours.'

'D'you mind if I take a look?'

(Bates then addresses Miss Wood.) 'What do you think of the facilities that we offer on DBC?'

'It seems to be very . . . comprehensive. Seems to cover all angles.'

(Bates now directs his gaze at all three.) 'I should mention to you that we've got a rate that includes all meals and if it's not possible to take them on the property – naturally I appreciate that the some of the crew are out a lot – then a suitable packed meal is provided.'

'What rate are we talking about as an average, Mr Bates?'

(Bates passes a sheet of paper to each of them. After studying the figures, Miss Hills turns to Bates.) 'Mmm . . . a little more than what we're typically paying with the contract rates that we've been getting from certain properties, but then . . . Mmm . . . I suppose we're talking about something that's a bit different, maybe.'

'Yes, indeed. Do you mind if I ask, Miss Hills, what happens with the crew as far as meals go in other places you've used.'

'Well, they tend to eat in the hotel and if the hotel doesn't have the capacity they'll go out somewhere. Naturally, it's all on expenses.'

'Does that sometimes lead to you going over budget on certain productions?'

'*Sometimes!* I wish that were so. More likely *all the time*!'

'So you've got no control on their spending when they eat in the hotels, if they can, and also when they're out? I suppose there's all those taxis as well.'

'That's true.'

'So if you paid a slightly higher rate with us, which includes meals, then it probably works out the same as the figure you're used to – or probably even less, I imagine.'

'Yes, less I would say, looking at the restaurant bills I have to sign off!'

'So you'd get better cost control and also your crew would get guaranteed seating in the hotel for their meals and wouldn't have the inconvenience of having to go out.'

'Sounds good – keep them under control!'

Twenty minutes later, after Bates had left, Mr Hitchcock, Holly Wood and Beverley Hills discuss the meeting:

'That was very interesting.'

'Yes. I think we can use them a lot. They've got some great properties in just our kinds of locations.'

'And those rates aren't bad at all, really. With the meals thrown in, our bottom-line figures could look a lot healthier.'

'Yeah, and the clients might then give us some leeway with those other things we've been suggesting to them. Could be good. I liked that chap . . . Blake – no, what am I talking about Holly – was it Blake? Age, you know – creeps up.'

'No, Mr Hitchcock. You'll have to use a memory technique like mine – "association", the "psychos" call it – I just think of the Bates Motel!'

Have you developed ESP?

Questionnaire

Check your empathy rating with this questionnaire. (Answers and a scoring scale on page 181.)

1 What do you understand by the term 'empathy'? is it:
   (a) A shampoo
   (b) The ability to change somebody's mind
   (c) Seeing things as other people do, and feeling with them
   (d) Not pushing too hard

2 As you enter your boss's office, you see that she has just put down a bottle of tablets after swallowing two or more of these. She apologises as she greets you. You note that the bottle is marked 'Paracetamol'. Do you:
   (a) Assume everything is OK, since she hasn't brought up the subject in the first five minutes
   (b) Ask her if she's trying to end it all
   (c) Show concern and offer to reschedule the meeting if she's suffering discomfort
   (d) Tell her you know of a more powerful and effective analgesic

3 Tests show that we speak at roughly how many words per minute:
   (a) 100–150
   (b) 400–600
   (c) 800–1000
   (d) 1000–1200

4 You meet a friend in the evening and she looks preoccupied. She reveals that she's got some problems at work, without going into any details of what they are. Do you:
   (a) Try to alter her mood by telling her not to worry and to 'cheer up'
   (b) Not refer to her problems, so that they become prominent in her mind and ruin the evening

(c) Ask an 'open' question such as: 'How do you feel they treat you at work?'

(d) Ask a 'closed' question, such as: 'Do you like working for them?'

5 You're with a prospective client. The secretary walks in with some tea. She puts your cup on the edge of her boss's desk on top of some of his papers. Do you:

(a) Leave things as they are (after all, *she* didn't consider it a problem)

(b) Leave the tea and pretend you only drink vodka

(c) Finish the tea and then move the empty cup away, if possible

(d) Remove it instantly and place it somewhere where it's not doing any harm, making sure the client sees your actions

6 Tests show that we think at roughly how many words per minute?

(a) 800–1000

(b) 100–150

(c) 450–600

(d) 1000–1500

7 You're telephoning one of your clients about something that's important to you. When you get through, she asks if you wouldn't mind keeping it short, as she's in a meeting. Do you:

(a) Get it over with quickly

(b) Ask her lots of questions so that it will (you hope) prolong the call in a natural manner

(c) Tell her that you'll write to her

(d) Suggest that as she's busy you'd much prefer to call her later in the day or another day, if she would give you a specific time and date when she'll be free

8 In the middle of a face-to-face meeting, your client's telephone rings. He apologises and takes the call. While he's speaking, do you:

(a) Look at him and smile constantly

(b) Make a signal to him and sneak out to go to the toilet or chat to the secretary or receptionist

(c) Turn your gaze away from him and perhaps occupy yourself with some papers or make some notes

(d) Use body language to show your impatience so that he knows you are busy too, hoping it will make him hurry up

9   The director of your Australian subsidiary, Mr Brown, is in the
    UK. He's accompanying you on a visit to one of your important
    clients, Mr Johnson. When you fixed the meeting two weeks
    ago, Mr Johnson mentioned he knew the town in Australia that
    your colleague hailed from.

    At the meeting, your director says to Mr Johnson: 'I under-
    stand you know my home town.' After some hesitation, Mr
    Johnson, responds with a weak 'Yes' and changes the subject.

    It's obvious to you that your client has forgotten you ever
    discussed Mr Brown's home town, and is trying to hide his
    embarrassment. What's more, you can almost see the wheels
    turning in his head as he desperately tries to remember: he's not
    concentrating on what you're saying. Do you:
    (a) Decide not to worry about it – it's not important now
    (b) Try and slip a note to your client reminding him of the
         name of the town
    (c) Subtly introduce the name in some way so that it's not
         obvious to either party: e.g., 'Don's a bit of a legend in
         Kangahogan; he's been known to . . .'
    (d) Say to Mr Johnson: 'You do remember Don's home town,
         don't you?'

10 You're in a restaurant entertaining a client. The tables are
    very close together. At a certain point your discussion turns to
    something quite confidential. Conversation has lagged on the
    table next to you, and your client's manner suggests that she's
    reluctant to speak. Do you:
    (a) Start speaking in a hushed voice and hope that she'll
         respond *sotto voce*
    (b) Look sideways and stare at the people on the next table,
         hoping your body language will tell them to start talking
         among themselves
    (c) Summon the manager and ask him to turn up the music
    (d) Try and change the subject until the coast is clear
    (e) Ignore the silence on the next table and continue the
         discussion, but decide to boycott the restaurant in future
         because of the seating problem

11 A potential client keeps looking at his watch surreptitiously
    during your discussion. He doesn't think you've spotted this,
    but, for the last thirty minutes, it's been distracting you and
    preventing you giving your best. What do you do:
    (a) Hurriedly bring your presentation to a close

   (b) Just ignore it; it might be a nervous mannerism or an obsessive–compulsive disorder

   (c) Stop talking at each point that he looks at his watch

   (d) Ask him politely: 'How long have we got?'

12 A potential client asks you to telephone him with a proposal (following a meeting) as soon as you have formulated it. You telephone on Friday at 9.30 am. His secretary says he'll be out of a meeting at around 4 pm and alerts you to the fact that he'll be leaving at 4.30 to visit someone in hospital. Do you:

   (a) Leave the details with the secretary

   (b) Call him at the hospital

   (c) Call him at 4.25 pm

   (d) Call him on Monday

   (e) Call him at 4 pm

13 You promise a client that the next time you meet you'll bring him a rare copy of an early Superman comic for his son. You forget this the next time you meet at his office.

However, as you are leaving and walking past a telephone box (association?!), you suddenly remember. Do you:

   (a) Assume he's forgotten all about the comic, since he didn't mention it (besides, you'd like to hang on to it; could be worth something, come to think of it)

   (b) Make sure you remember it the next time you see your client

   (c) Telephone him and say that you haven't forgotten about the comic and you'll get it to him very soon

   (d) To save face, tell him the next time you meet that it's been stolen

14 You've discovered your red felt-tip pen has leaked and there's a lot of ink showing down the front of your shirt. As you enter the interviewer's office, your mind is on how to conceal this. Do you:

   (a) Hope she won't notice

   (b) Keep your arms folded at all times

   (c) Explain on arrival what's happened, and make fun of your carelessness

   (d) Cancel the interview

15 The golden rule for effective presentation and maximising attention is (fill in the blanks):

Say what _ _ _ _ _ going _ _   _ _ _

Say _ _

Say _ _ _ _ you _ _ _ _

16 After a long meeting with a potential client, during which she insisted on covering all the nitty-gritty in your literature and fine print, she agrees to a trial subscription. Your forms contain many terms and conditions. You notice the inscription on her coffee mug: 'What the large print giveth, the small print taketh away!'. To wrap things up, do you:
   (a) Produce the form and go through each item with her
   (b) Ask her to confirm in writing (preferably for you to take away with you); you can then send an official form on to her with an acknowledgement
   (c) Make an exception with this client and accept a verbal 'handshake agreement'
   (d) Ask for payment in advance (in cash!)

17 You're introduced to three new people, and miss one of the names. What do you do?
   (a) Decide not to worry – two out of three isn't bad
   (b) Ask him: 'Sorry, I didn't catch your name'
   (c) Guess
   (d) Ask one of the other two people his name, when he's distracted

18 The secretary walks into her boss's office during the meeting you're having with him and tells him: 'Mr Scott said could you give him a buzz on 421 within the next ten minutes. He said it's urgent and he'll be going out soon.' Do you:
   (a) Accelerate your talk so as to be finished within seven or eight minutes
   (b) Tell him that there is no way you can be expected to finish your presentation in a few minutes and that you hadn't realised there'd be such a time constraint
   (c) Politely suggest that he may like to sort out the call now, while you occupy yourself with some paperwork
   (d) Wait for him to say something, and, if he doesn't, just carry on where you left off

19 What does 'psycholinguistics' mean? Is it:
   (a) An aerobic exercise from California
   (b) The study of how celluloid thrillers affect the mind
   (c) How certain words affect our minds and emotions

20 You have to write to a client following a meeting in which you were negotiating your fee. The figure you quoted at the meeting was £15,800. You'd agreed before you left that, by making certain changes, this could be reduced to £14,900. The client wanted £14,000. You have worked out that £14,400 is the lowest you can go to. How is your letter phrased?

(a) 'Unfortunately, £14,400 is the lowest figure . . .'
(b) 'So I'm afraid the lowest figure we can go to would be £14,400'
(c) 'We're happy to say that we'll work with you at the reduced fee of £14,400'
(d) 'You said at the meeting that you would give the OK at a figure of £14,000 . . . We can go to £14,400'

21 When you're with friends or with somebody in a work situation, and you hand them something to read, do you:
(a) Decide to make it easy for them by giving them a running commentary as they're reading
(b) Ask them to wake you up when they've finished
(c) Remain silent

22 Do you appreciate the value of silence in a social or work situation, when appropriate words or facts are not forthcoming? If you do, then correctly fill in the blanks in this ancient proverb:
    'Better to keep your _ _ _ _ _ shut and be thought a _ _ _ _, than to _ _ _ _ it and remove all _ _ _ _ _ !

23 You're going on holiday to Tuscany this year, and you're moving house in the autumn. During your conversation with a client, he reveals that he himself is off to Florence the next weekend. When he returns from holiday, he is away for a further two weeks because he is moving house.
    He suggests you get in touch with him again after two months, when the dust has settled. You don't rate yourself as having a good memory, but there are two pieces of information which you must have registered (through association) and should not fail to use when you meet this person again. Which two?
(a) He was a man
(b) The last time you met, he was going to Florence
(c) He wore spectacles
(d) He was moving house

24 'From the moment I picked up this book, till the moment I put it down, I was convulsed with laughter. Someday I intend to read it!' (Groucho Marx) – Which book was Groucho referring to?

(a) *The Power of Positive Thinking*, by Norman Vincent Peale
(b) *Men are from Mars and Women are from Venus*, by John Gray
(c) *The Inner Game of Selling Yourself*, by James Borg
(d) *A Christmas Carol*, by Charles Dickens
(e) None of these books

25 Justin Case left his home at the same time every day. As an occupational psychologist, he worked in offices in the centre of London, travelling into town on the same underground train every morning. He caught his crowded train that morning, as usual, where the twenty minute journey was to be spent standing huddled up with others in this regrettable but accepted invasion of one's personal space 'bubble'.

While he was aware of the importance of making eye contact in social and work situations, he didn't think this extended to observing fellow travellers at close quarters. The dishevelled man standing next to him obviously did. His constant touching of the face and other nervous non-verbal signals proved an irritant to Justin Case. He decided that this fellow who was staring at him suspiciously deserved a rebuff. So he turned a half-circle and was faced with a much better proposition in the form of a very pretty brunette.

At the next station, the train came to a sudden stop and a few passengers lost their balance, including the man with the staring eyes. He fell on Justin Case, grabbing hold of the lapels of his finely tailored jacket. It was deliberate, concluded Case, as he fixed a disapproving stare at the man, who now semed to be trying to wade through the packed train towards the sliding doors.

Justin Case brushed an imaginary fleck off his shoulder, flattened his lapels and attempted to straighten his tie. As he was patting his jacket, he subconsciously registered that the normal bulge in his inside pocket was not evident.

His wallet. *It had gone.*

His thoughts immediately turned to the fleeing man, who was frantically trying to get to the doors of the train at the other end of the carriage. Of course, that's what he was up to, he thought.

'Stop him! Stop him! Thief!' he shouted as astonished faces looked up from newspapers – and then looked down again. He called to a man who seemed to be having a serious business conversation on his mobile phone ('Yes, I'm on the train . . .

about another eight minutes . . . yes, it's dark in the tunnel . . . Well, corned beef and tomato is my preference – not too much mustard, mind you . . .') trying to interrupt his conversation to get him to dial 999.

The thief was just getting off the train, and the automatic doors had started to close. Case leapt to the doors and just about managed to grab the culprit's tie as the doors closed.

'Stop the train somebody – stop the train!' he shouted – but it had already started to move. He held on to the man's tie. The thief started waving his arms and cursing, and was pulled along as the train started moving faster. His head was banging along the side of the doors and blood started to appear all over his face. Some of the women passengers screamed. 'Let him go!' they shouted at Case, but he hung on to the man's tie as the train sped along. 'He's got my wallet,' snarled Case, justifying his iron-like grip on the man's tie.

The thief was looking in a sorry state as blood covered the glass. 'We're going into the tunnel now,' a man in a bowler hat shouted, pointing the tip of his umbrella towards the oncoming tunnel.

Luckily for the thief, his tie snapped in Case's hands. He was left clutching half a tie. The bloodstained man was left staggering on the platform.

Justin Case cursed himself. 'I nearly had him,' he thought. 'Why didn't I notice what he was up to before?'

The train pulled up at the next station and Case got out of the carriage. He was due to go straight to a client meeting that morning, but there was no possibility of attending that: his hands were grazed and bloodstained. He walked to the telephone booth. Drat! His phone card and also his client's number were in the wallet. 'Never mind,' he proudly thought to himself, 'I've memorised my PIN number for my telephone chargecard (using my unique memory system) and my client's telephone number. He felt rather pleased at being able to recall these important numbers, his first feeling of positive emotion that day.

Case spoke to his clients, explained what had happened, and told them that he was on his way to his own offices now and would give them a call to reschedule the 'focus group' morning for another day.

He got into a taxi and after recounting the story to the inquisitive taxi driver, eventually arrived at his destination. He walked up the stairs and entered his office, where he was greeted by his shocked secretary, Miss Anthrope.

'Are you all right, Mr Case? What on earth has happened to you?'

'Oh, nothing. Don't worry. I've got to reschedule this morning's meeting with McCain Taylor. Could you get my diary Miss Anthrope?'

'Oh, by the way, Mr Case. Your wife called.'

'Did she leave any message?'

'Yes. She said . . .'

What was the message from Case's wife? (The answer is worth ten points.)

Answers

1 (a) 0
  (b) −5
  (c) 10 (Interestingly, the Greek origin of the word means 'to feel pain with'.)
  (d) 0

2 (a) 1 Most people wouldn't.
  (b) −5
  (c) 5 More likely than not she'll be unable to give you worthwhile attention. Her mind will be on how to shorten the meeting.
  (d) 2

3 (a) 5 Right answer
  (b) 0
  (c) −2
  (d) −5

4 (a) 1
  (b) 0
  (c) 5
  (d) 3

5 (a) 0 It isn't *her* problem
  (b) 0
  (c) 5 He can concentrate on listening to you now instead of worrying about his papers.
  (d) 3

6 (a) 1
  (b) −2
  (c) 5 Right answer. (Remember: we can think at roughly *four times* the rate at which somebody is speaking. Small wonder that we have to work hard to detect and prevent loss of attention from our audience!)
  (d) 0

7 (a) 1
  (b) −5 She hasn't got the time or the inclination right now. She's distracted; she's got people with her, and she's keeping them waiting. If you're not careful and you push it, she'll impress them by the assertive act of getting rid of you.
  (c) 1
  (d) 5 This gives you a better chance of achieving your goal.

8 (a) −2 Give him some breathing space. Don't stare at him! And what are you smiling at anyway. It can be off-putting to the person on the phone.
  (b) −4
  (c) 5 You're making him feel comfortable now. It's in your interest; he's secretly thanking you for it. *Quelle* empathy!
  (d) −5

9 (a) 0
  (b) 1
  (c) 5 You've embarrassed neither of the parties; you've been subtle – they probably don't know what you've been trying to do. Even if the client guesses, he can't be sure. Besides, he's now more comfortable: he can engage in natural conversation.
  (d) −5 Don't make him lose face.

10 (a) 2
   (b) 1
   (c) −4
   (d) 5
   (e) −5 This won't help you at the moment. Bad seating is a common fault in many restaurants and hotels. Make sure you choose a good table in the first place if you're discussing confidential matters.

11 (a) 0
   (b) 1
   (c) −1
   (d) 5 You should find out the real problem this way.

12 (a) −3
   (b) −10
   (c) −5
   (d) 5 You should get a better reception. Also, he's got an uninterrupted working week to concentrate on your proposal, rather than a weekend to dilute its impact.
   (e) −2 Will he be in the mood to talk to you then?

13 (a) −5

(b) 1 There might not *be* a next time now.

(c) 10 No time like the present. The client had been disturbed during the meeting because of your empty promise. He'd told his son about the 'gift', and was doubting your sincerity.

(d) −10

14 (a) −5 The distraction would be too great. The interviewer would be wondering if your bullet-proof vest had failed; or was it clumsiness with a tomato-ketchup bottle? But, more importantly, she'd be dying to know if *you* knew about the stain.

(b) −4

(c) 5 At least she knows that you know. Also, there's an explanation: you're not just a slob!

(d) 0 Can you really spare the time to do this?

15 Say what you're going to say,
Say it.
Say what you said.
(5 points for the correct answer)

16 (a) −2 If she's that pedantic it may make her change her mind. She may want to hold off and study it carefully.

(b) 5 She's committed herself in her own mind now.

(c) −5

(d) 0

17 (a) −1 No excuse. He could be the most important member of the group.

(b) 5 Now you're talking!

(c) −10 Worse than no name – the *wrong* name!

(d) 2

18 (a) −5

(b) 2 If you're going to take this line, be polite.

(c) 5 At least he'll be able to concentrate on you now.

(d) −1 He may spring an abrupt 'thank you for coming' after five minutes (before you've finished).

19 (a) −5

(b) −5

(c) 5

20 (a) −4 'Unfortunately . . .' You're planting negative vibes in the other person's mind. Why?

(b) −5 So I'm afraid . . .' Ugh!

(c) 5 You've turned negative vibes into positive ones. Bravo! And you're offering exactly the same deal.

(d) −10 Don't remind him of this. He's probably forgotten that he ever said it.

21 (a) −4 Can anyone really concentrate on two things at once?

(b) −5

(c) 5

22 'Better to keep your mouth shut and be thought a fool, than to open it and remove all doubt!'
(5 points for the correct answer)

23 (a) −5

(b) 5

(c) −4

(d) 5

If you can't programme your mind to remember (b) and (d), which are common to you both, empathy skills and memory techniques need to be sharpened up *considerably*.

24 (a) 0

(b) 0

(c) −10 You cannot be *serious*!

(d) 0

(e) 5 Groucho wasn't referring to any of them – so please feel free to recommend *this* book to your friends and colleagues!

25 'Yes. She said you left your wallet at home.'

Scoring scale

130 to 140: This book must have done you some good. Empathy, sincerity, perspicacity – you're displaying all three. Please keep it up.

100 to 129: You're developing ESP by the minute.

75 to 99: Nearly there.

50 to 74: A few weak areas that need working on.

21 to 49: Come *on* – get inside the mind!

5 to 20 Please read the book again

−100 to 4: *Don't answer any more questions without checking with your lawyer!*